And Another Thing...

Reflections from My Small Town

To Sharon and Pam
Thanks!
Susan Rushton

SUSAN RUSHTON

ISBN: 978-0-9885552-2-8
Library of Congress Control Number: 2012923700
Literary Collections/Essays

All material originally appeared 1987-2012 in the *Auburn Journal,* a publication
    of Gold Country Media—a division of Brehm Communications, Inc.,
    P.O. Box 28429, San Diego, CA 92198-0429 (auburnjournal.com,
    goldcountrymedia.com, brehmcommunications.com)

Published in the United States of America by Mootpoint Press, P.O. Box
    3362, Auburn CA 95604: mootpointpress.com
Cover art by Michael Kirby: kirbyphoto.net
Cover design and Mootpoint Press logo by Vance Sauter, Golden Triangle
    Publications: goldtrippub.com

mootpointpress.com

Dedication

To my readers. You know who you are. So do I. What a pleasure.

To my several editors at the *Auburn Journal*. Thanks, friends.

To Anne Whitson. She handed me my first copy of *Writers' Digest* when I was 10 years old. She may not remember, but I do. So this is all your fault, Annie.

To Gloria Beverage. This is all your fault, too. Tag, girl, you're it.

To my writing students. Thanks for keeping me honest. Any specific example is here because of you.

To my writing groups. Thanks for keeping me honest. Any specific example is here because of you.

To Don. Thanks for keeping me honest. Any specific example is here because... no, wait. That's not it. Here: you're the purple light of a summer night in Spain.

Table of Contents

Introduction

YOU MIGHT NOT know about Auburn, my small town. But I'm not sure whether it matters. Once I thought it did. Once I thought Auburn—its back roads and 19th century buildings, quirky individuals, its evolving downtown and profound sense of community, all of it, including its Northern Californianess—was unique. I know many people here think so.

I also know that many people who have never heard of Auburn feel this way about their own towns, their communities or neighborhoods. Granted, your town is unique because you live there. It has its own history, its own stories, its own traditions.

Yet in spite of our individual fingerprints, we are all human. I'm convinced that if I feel or think a certain way, or wonder something, so do others.

So if you, too, live in a town with good neighbors and grumpy neighbors, if you haunt a coffee shop haunted by various (other) eccentric characters, if your newspaper carries boisterous letters to the editor, if your City Council raises eyebrows occasionally, you live in a town like Auburn. How fortunate you are.

My husband Don and I arrived in 1985. Almost the moment we got here, I approached the *Auburn Journal* and its editor, the late A. Thomas Homer. Want a book review? I asked. Sure, A. Thomas said.

I gave him one. To my astonishment, I saw it in the paper the next day. With a byline and everything.

So I hung around. Tom didn't discourage me. Yes, he rolled his eyes at me, but he kept offering me assignments, and I kept accepting them. I loved those bylines!

In 1987, between researching Placer County towns and entering birth announcements, I submitted some light, column-like pieces. Those found their way into a few special sections. Ah! More bylines!

Finally, in 1989, the paper gave me space for my own weekly opinion column: *And Another Thing.*

I love *And Another Thing.* It keeps me on my toes, encourages me to pay attention, forces me to hone my writing skills. I love the feedback I get.

I left the paper at the end of 1991, but the column stayed. After 25 years, I have decided to collect a bunch of my favorites. All of these have previously appeared in the *Auburn Journal.*

I don't always—or even necessarily—focus on Auburn, as you'll see quite clearly quite soon. On the other hand, I reflect on my world from my small town. Living here colors my view.

I've organized the book in very general sections. Sometimes the themes overlap, as with Rufus T. Firefly or Ms. Mootpoint. Politics raises its ugly head there as well as in, well, Politics. Funny stuff appears peppered in various places as well as in Humor. Finally, within each section, I present the columns in chronological order.

I have picked at and picked through every column I've included. Made each better, in other words. If something isn't exactly the way you remember it—if you remember it—that's why.

Please enjoy. Thanks for reading.

one

Relentless Optimism

T HE SILVER LINING that keeps popping up in my columns continues
to surprise me. My insistence on looking for that silver lining surprises me.
Yes, I seethe and slobber and rant and rave. I imagine you do, too. But
when ranting gets old, I gaze at the late afternoon sun through the tops of the
oaks.

When I get tired of venting my rage at whatever or whoever it is that deserves
that rage, I take comfort in the laughter I share with Don, or the taste of sourdough bread or my delight in an elegantly-written sentence—my own or somebody else's.

And we agree, you and I, that those three tasty ingredients in a full life
represent only a few of many on a delicious, unending list. Yes, we find a lot to
be mad at, but we find a lot to love as well. That doesn't surprise me at all.

Listen for the Song of the Lark

I N MY LIVING room, I have a print of a painting called *Song of the Lark*. In it, the 19th century painter Jules Breton gives me a barefoot young woman at sunrise, laboring in the field with a sickle. She's stopped in her tracks.

I imagine that a moment before, she was bent over the earth—but now she stands straight and her face carries a look of wonder and joy. Not at what she sees, but at what she hears.

In the sky above her, tiny and hard to see, is what she listens to with such intensity: a lark.

OK, fine, so she listens to a lark. But consider: She lives in the late 1800s, is a peasant and a woman, pretty much a rotten combination.

Maybe one of 13 children, she probably cannot read or write, has no money of her own and never will. She has no dowry, so nobody's beating down her father's door. Next year she'll marry a man a couple of sections over who has nothing much to offer her, either, except the willingness to marry her.

If bearing children doesn't kill her, she'll spend her life divided between scraping the earth and raising those children, over half of whom will die before they're five.

What harshness… but surrounded by it, in spite of it, she allows herself to pay attention to beauty. It means something to her.

She is caught by the song of the lark.

News always seems to present the grim side, the serial killers, the side with the homeless, asbestos poisoning and oil spills. All the neon arrows point to the negative.

It sells papers, but it's not healthy.

Sure, there's misery in the world, but there's also brightness and warmth. So few are encouraged to look at it. So few decide to look for it.

Yes, there's very little we can count on, there will always be deception and treachery, we all die. But in spite of the mess in the Balkans, there are the elegant faces of tigers and the intense voice of jazz singer Joe Williams.

Yes, there are bad cops but there are also good cops. Consider opposable thumbs, Jack Benny, the chambered nautilus, the mottled white bark of sycamores in winter.

Terrorists blow up airliners, but this same world also boasts the movies of Michael Curtiz, Howard Hawks and Alfred Hitchcock; and the paintings of Georgia O'Keefe, the poetry of John Keats, the statues of Michelangelo.

Plus good sex. Even—you know—not-so-bad sex. And the slide trombone. Rachmaninoff's piano concertos. The smell of bay leaves. The speed of the peregrine falcon and moonlight on water.

Or the three-six-three double play.

Sure, you can discount these things, focus only on the appalling, but how does it help? What good does it do?

After a while, the appalling tends to paralyze people. It convinces those who focus on it that there's no hope, that pessimism is the only reasonable response.

If I focus solely on the negative, I no longer see the sun dappling through the trees in the late afternoons, or wind blowing foam off the tops of ocean waves or the favors done for me by dear friends.

Ignoring the idiocy and the tragedy is no good either, but certainly there's middle ground. There is. I've found it.

In the midst of grimness, people need to listen for and listen to any larks that might be around. All right, all right, so I'm Pollyanna. But those larks are there, and it's reassuring and healthy to find them. It's even better to consciously search for them. Because the more you look, the more you find.

They exist. I've seen them. I suggest you look for them, too.

###

April 26, 1989

FYI: Over lunch a while ago, Gloria Beverage, my friend and former coworker in the Journal *newsroom, challenged me to publish a collection of my columns. She said she had a particular fondness for one of my earliest ones—the one about the painting of that peasant girl who lets the song of the lark interrupt her work in the field. I didn't plan it this way, but I'm happy to offer it first in this book.*

Taking Risks

S HE FIDGETED ON the edge of the high dive for long moments, vaguely aware of her shouting, taunting companions clustered around the ladder below. Uppermost in her mind was how high she was and what a risk she was taking by what she planned: jumping into the pool.

It was terrible: so high, so far away.

Yet she had talked herself into it. She had made the commitment—either moments or hours before—and had gotten as far as the edge of this too-springy plank nine (nine!) feet above the water.

She had two choices. She could change her mind and climb down. Or she could go forward. Both seemed impossible. She felt caught between shouts of derision or stepping into the unknown.

But she knew that lots of people had performed this risky act, several of whom she heard shrieking at her to hurry up—so it was safe.

Safe? Oh, sure. If she were safe, she wouldn't feel this way.

I, too, was vaguely aware of her companions. Some fidgeted next to me, trying to get my attention. But they could wait. Her moment of truth was more important.

The last instant before she stepped off the board she looked at me, so far away in the bleachers—*so* far away. So dry and so grown up. So safe. Electricity passed between us. I understood, and I knew she knew I understood.

Finally, too soon and at last, she stepped into the air.

She was 10 years old, and this was 18 years ago, my first year of teaching. I wonder if Julie remembers that moment as clearly as I do.

Risk, clearly, is a relative thing.

I've driven cross-country by myself, a relatively risky thing to do. I've stepped off the edge of the high dive of relationships and dared to tell someone I care about him, which is a damn sight riskier than driving cross-country. I've stood gasping at the top of a mogully monster in the wind and fog and skied off the edge into the whiteness.

More recently, a coworker boasted that he'd spent the day before bungee jumping.

Jumping off a platform 200 feet above the water, connected to security by glorified rubber bands—the idea titillated the younger, more single denizens of the building.

Illegal? Dangerous? Terrifying? Well, sure. But what interested them most was giving their adrenal glands the opportunity to perform.

The rewards of something like bungee jumping are predictable: goosebumps, your heart in your mouth and roaring in your ears. And adrenaline's searing heat radiating everywhere at once.

What's not predictable is yourself at that moment of stepping off the edge, whether it's the high dive, the too-small platform available to bungee-jumpers—or whatever stands with you at that edge dividing familiarity from the unexplored, the unknown.

And there's never any end to what's unexplored.

Years ago, about the time I sat in the bleachers and watched Julie on the high dive, I found a quote by Goethe that touched me considerably:

"What you can do, or dream you can, begin it," went the translation from the German. "Courage has genius, power and magic in it."

Yes. I put that on and it fit just fine.

Julie's courage fit her just fine, too. After her jump she burst to the surface, thrilled beyond all expectation. After another electric look between us, she raced unafraid to the high dive to try it again.

June 14, 1991

FYI: Or: "Do the thing you think you cannot do."—Eleanor Roosevelt

Picture from Life

I DON'T HAVE the picture anymore. But I did once, had it for years, and I looked at it so often that I don't believe it matters that it's gone.

On this full page from *Life* magazine, bars of some sort dominate the immediate foreground. This close up, I can't tell whether this is a fence, prison bars or a window. The primary impression, though, is one of restriction.

The background, mostly gray and white and black, is indistinct. It could be anything—maybe smoke, maybe fog. Especially out of focus this way.

In the center, back there beyond the bars, against that fuzzy background, an equally fuzzy figure in a red sweater jumps, his arms high, legs bent under him. I like to think he leaps just for the hell of it, because he likes it, likes the feeling of being in midair for a moment.

Now—is he confined? If he is, does he care? Does he brood over the walls surrounding him? It doesn't look like it. The walls don't seem to affect him at all. He behaves as if they don't exist. He's having fun, doing what he wants.

I looked at that photo and something clicked. Shoving this increasingly creased picture at everyone I knew, I made a pest of myself for weeks afterward.

Look, I pestered. *What do you see? What are those bars? What's going on? Why's he jumping?*

At that time, I kept hearing people screaming about the restrictions placed on us. All these laws, all these bureaucrats telling us what we can and can't do, society straitjacketing us, insisting we conform, conform, conform, so we're all like so many houses in a tract.

Restraints placed on us by law enforcement, the government, marriage and employers, I heard, prevent us from doing what we want, from making our own decisions and choosing our own way.

Rumors spread through the underground about a newfangled, high-tech listening device that detected conversations from some horribly long distance away. Worse, it deciphered words merely by gauging the sound vibrations hitting a window. *Big Brother's everywhere,* rose the cry.

I hear the same complaint today, only more often. Private citizens have no privacy. We're observed, followed and categorized with our every move, and we've become constrained and shackled as a result.

Yet I find I'm having a pretty good time, in spite of all this shackling, if that is in fact what's going on. Sure, there are plenty of things I can't do. I can't drive over the speed limit. I must refrain from poisoning—even maiming—my neighbor if we disagree. I need to follow instructions if I want insurance coverage.

But life itself puts constraints on me. Should I drink as much as I might want to, my body rebels the next day. I can't jump 10 feet because gravity prevents me. I will only live a certain number of years. But naïvely, in spite of all these barriers, I'm enjoying myself.

That boy jumping in the photograph might be naïve, too, but look at him. Although behind bars he insists on happiness in spite of them, ignores them, refusing to let them curb his joy. Because he ignores the bars, they don't exist.

What if he focused only on the bars? Then those barriers would surround him, and his whole consciousness would remain in darkness, allowing those barriers to prevent him from—well, just prevent him. Would he find the light-heartedness to jump then? The optimism? Would he feel *free* to jump?

Now—you might find fault with my perspective, and point out that I may be the one behind bars, not him. OK. Fair enough. If that's the case, I choose to look at that kid in the red sweater, leaping out of delight, just because he can and feels like it. I pay attention to someone enjoying himself. Which makes me happy.

It's a matter of vision: what you choose to focus on. Concentrate on the bars, and the bars catch you, paralyze you—and you're doomed. Concentrate on joy, and there's where life is. Rejoice!

March 27, 1992

The More Things Change...

A FTER EVERYONE LEFT the meeting in the old school-room, I yielded to my curiosity and pulled open the world map I'd wondered about for an hour.

Finally I got a good look at all these odd, old countries: Belgian Congo, French Indochina, Siam, Italian East Africa, Netherland Indonesia. And seeing those, I knew I wouldn't find any of the new-fangled places like Bangladesh, Pakistan or Moldova, Laos, Zimbabwe, Vietnam or Somalia. Korea was still a single country. Germany hadn't been divided—or united—yet.

What a find. Some of these countries no longer existed. Here was an Africa arrogantly carved up and arbitrarily claimed by Italy, England, France, Portugal and Belgium.

How old was this map? I hunted for a copyright date, but found none. I had ways of pinning down its approximate age, though. It was Palestine, not Israel, that hunched there next to Jordan on the edge of the Mediterranean Sea. My first clue: This map was at least 45 years old.

But of course, it had to be older than that, because Germany didn't get divided until 1945. And nobody'd be so foolhardy as to update world maps during a world war, right? So probably—no later than 1939?

And since I found Leningrad, known as Petrograd until it was renamed in 1924, it was no older than 70.

Wow, I thought. *The world's sure changed over the past seven decades.*

Almost immediately, I revised my conclusion. *No, the world hasn't changed,* I corrected myself, *only the maps have.* Only the lines on these political divisions sorted out by officials and policy makers— they're the only things that change.

The lines in the dust, the scratches in the sand, they move one foot or seven miles to the east or west, north or south. People may choose to follow them, depending on where those lines move, but does that change the world? Not much.

In the decades since that map was printed, people haven't changed much, either. The racism implied by the European colonialism of Africa still exists. The violence implied by England's occupation of India still exists, too, and the willingness to resort to force rather than intellect and reason.

Greed, sexism, cruelty, intolerance of another's religion, drug abuse—they all existed then and they all exist now. Ugliness has always existed.

But since we haven't changed much over those few decades, I know that the dedication, kindness, generosity of heart, courage and energy I see in my friends and in strangers I pass and in people I read about—these things haven't changed, either.

Strangers laugh over a shared quick joke, and although they remain strangers, they part warmly. Friends gather to support one another in trouble. I share a confidence, and the person I tell it to keeps it to himself. I smile at a new mother, and she smiles back as I touch her newborn's hand.

None of this is new. This wonderful, kind behavior exists now—

and it always has. To my delight, I find it everywhere.

The lines in the sand these days—Croatia, Serbia, the restoration of countries now free of Soviet domination—are just that, lines in the sand. People behave as they always have. This can serve as depressing news. After all, shouldn't we have learned anything from English colonialism, from the Nazis, from the Khmer Rouge, from our own Jim Crow days?

But at the same time, because people's behavior hasn't changed, individuals—just as they always have—perform stunning acts of sacrifice and friendship, courage and patience and tolerance. People keep promises. People prove that they deserve trust. You see this happening all around you.

A line shifting in the sand is news. Man's inhumanity to man is old news, but it's news.

Man's *humanity* to man is old news too, but it isn't scandalous or hideous, so it's not publicized. *But I see it everywhere.* And because I keep seeing it, I have hope, because people haven't changed.

April 1, 1993

Slaves to Our Impulses?

H E TOILED QUIETLY at the recycled newspaper hut on Sacramento Street, near Fairgate and Auburn-Folsom. I stop there on my fairly regular trips to Auburn Community Recycling.

After I finish dropping off glass and aluminum, I leave my bags of newspaper at that little hut.

I hadn't seen him before. This day, though, I pulled up in front of his car and dragged out my sacrifices to the newsprint gods. Before me, the bulky bags spilled out of the hut and into the side road like drunken derelicts.

Dressed in slacks and a decent shirt, surrounded by a mess of paper, he shoved, dragged, stuffed and wrestled the piles into some semblance of sturdy order.

At least into more order.

He asked me to just set my bags down rather than toss them onto the stacks. He'd find a good place for them.

Responding to my questioning glance, he shrugged. "This needs organizing," he said. "So I organize it. Plus, relatives of mine live nearby and I didn't want them looking at this mess all the time."

I thanked him, trying somehow to tell him how much I appreciated his kind altruism and his unceasing, dirty, heavy work. People will always bring by their newspapers, because printing machines keep churning them out and people keep delivering them, day after day after day. This job made him a modern Sisyphus, the guy who kept pushing the boulder up the hill, only to have to start over when it inevitably rolled back down.

But he chafed at my appreciation. He was uncomfortable, even embarrassed. "It's no big deal," he muttered, avoiding my eyes.

Clearly, he wanted neither recognition nor gratitude for something he does because he wants to and because he believes it's the right thing to do.

So I did the next kindest thing. I shut up, gave him my papers and left.

Years ago, in 1984, a movie called *Impulse* came out. I didn't see it, but I did read a review of it. Something ugly happens in a small town and suddenly all the residents act out their impulses—robbing banks, urinating on cars, setting fire to utility companies.

The reviewer didn't like it. If people in this town suddenly succumb to their impulses, he asked, how come nobody does anything kind, generous or thoughtful? How come all their impulses are violent ones?

He knew the answer. So do you. Vicious impulses make for a better action movie. It's tough to smash up a ton of cars—or create much suspense—by keeping a promise or giving a baby a bath.

But ugliness doesn't reside alone inside us. It exists, of course. Consider, if you can stand it, the ongoing carnage in Rwanda and Bosnia.

I myself have some pretty ugly impulses. I even succumb to a few now and then.

But look around. If we're all just tools of our hostile impulses, then why are most of the windows you see on your street still all in one piece? It's been years, most likely, since your neighbor drove a front-end loader through your living room. And you can't recall the last time you sprayed your brother-in-law with ammonia while he trained his Dalmatian in the evening.

How come you don't barrel ahead of everybody in the grocery store? Why don't you make obscene phone calls at breakfast every morning? The fear of litigation or jail can't be all that's stopping you.

If our species is supposed to be so terrible, then such things as the Red Cross and Hospice, Kiwanis and public television, literacy programs, 50th wedding anniversaries, blood donors and knock-knock jokes shouldn't exist. To my delight, I see evidence of consideration and courtesy every day.

And I'll always cite as confirmation that man on Sacramento Street standing hip-deep in newsprint.

###

June 16, 1994

Hope for the World

I WANT TO tell you what encourages me, gives me hope for the world. Actually, a lot of things do. Toward the top of my list is the number of books published every year.

You're aware of the phenomenal success of the *Harry Potter* movie. This may seem a tad off the track, but not for long. You've heard about it: wham, right out of the starting gate, the biggest box office ever recorded. Huge numbers, gigantic popularity.

You're aware of it because of the insane media hype, all of it blaring at you in capital letters. Superlatives, that's all the major corporations look at and care about: the biggest numbers, the most popular. And when something goes over the top in such an overwhelming manner, well, you can bet the CEOs in high places notice. *Fantasy movies for children,* the big moguls mutter, scrambling frantically around their boardrooms, wracking their brains to find other surefire dynamos like Harry.

If the bottom line were all that matters, soon the only movies in theaters will be quirky fantasies about witches and wizards and spells.

Remember what came after *The Exorcist* in the 1970s? Maybe not. Well, suddenly the theaters crawled with devilish dramas.

Remember that success of any sort breeds imitation: *Texas Chainsaw Massacre* spawned a whole genre of grisly teen decapitation exploitation movies. *Nightmare on Elm Street. Halloween. Friday the 13th.*

And on and on. You know.

The thing is—and this is the thing that excites me—during those years, other kinds of movies turned up in theaters too. Directors and writers found other tales to tell, and told them well. Two years after *The Exorcist,* we had *Jaws, One Flew Over the Cuckoo's Nest* and *Dog Day Afternoon;* three years later, we had *All the President's Men, Rocky, Taxi Driver, Network, The Front* and *The Seven-Percent Solution.* And, of course, *The Omen.* But gee, consider all those others that had nothing to do with the dark side. Except, of course, for *All the President's Men.*

See? The extreme popularity of *The Exorcist* didn't spawn clones to the *nth* degree until you could only see that one genre in theatres.

Of course we'll have *Harry Potter* clones in a year or so. Sure we will—who doesn't want to rake in the dough? But we'll see more than just wizards. Even these days, with show biz tycoons straining for the big bucks, we'll have other movies.

Because somehow, to my delight, there's still a kind of wisdom around that caters to a variety of quirky tastes. Even those of us who avoid best sellers because they're best sellers have money to spend, and these guys know it.

That's what's so amazing about the book world. Publishers crank out thousands of titles every year, and most of them even the most devoted readers have never heard of. Certainly they never get around to reading them. Comparatively few books ever get on the *New York Times* Bestseller List, or even Amazon's.

Only a few receive the deafening attention given an Oprah pick, only a few get made into blockbuster movies *(Jaws, Harry Potter, Jurassic Park),* events that make the authors the darlings of Wall Street.

Yet a ton of quirky, charming, different, crazy, unusual, subtle, odd, sweet, clever books keep being published, books that may only attract a fraction (even a fraction of a fraction) of the readers who buy *Lord of the Rings*. It's thrilling that writers keep writing what comes into their heads, and that publishers continue throwing their books out there, even though most books aren't likely to haul in a ton of money.

Sure, authors like J.K. Rowling, J.R.R. Tolkien, John Grisham, James Patterson, Mary Higgins Clark and Stephen King tower above the rest of us like tyrannosaurus rex, but plenty of authors scramble around in the underbrush, authors who find enough to eat without making all that noise.

Jan. 3, 2002

More than One Ray of Hope

B AD NEWS, BAD news and worse news. Government and corporate incompetence, graft and stupidity—it seems endless, doesn't it? However, bear with me. Because I promise: I've uncovered a bright spot.

But first, here's a story about city government graft in *The Atlanta Constitution*. *The Detroit News* ferreted out a conspiracy in the Navy, where high mucky-mucks covered up reasons behind servicemen's deaths aboard ship. And what about all those stories in the *Seattle Times* about incompetence resulting in that ugly oil spill off the coast of Alaska?

I've recently researched Pulitzer Prize winners for a project at work. Last week I went through all the winners, from 1917 to 2001. At first, I only focused on the prize-winning authors of novels, history, poetry, drama—the literary stuff, people and works dear to my heart.

But at pulitzer.org, if you look at the winners by year, the pages list the media winners first: the newspapers. Of course. The press: That's where Pulitzer's heart lay. It's only after this serious stuff—breaking news, feature story, columnist, spot news photography winners—that they announce the other serious stuff I was originally looking for.

As I scrolled down, however, I kept being distracted by what papers had printed in, say, 1931, 1982 or 1990—the years those stories I begin this column with won the Pulitzer.

We realize, to our dismay, that government scandal and disgrace are not anomalies. In 1947, the *Baltimore Sun* uncovered ineptitude in Maryland's Unemployment Department, resulting in 93 convictions. In 1971, the *New York Times* published the Pentagon Papers, exposing the government's lies about our involvement in the Vietnam War and the complicity of four presidents.

And it keeps going. The tone of news published in 2002 is the same as that published 20, 40, or 70 years ago. The subject matter's no different: corrupt politicians, police brutality, vote tampering, immigrants living in squalor, education teetering on the precipice, cities falling apart, crooked corporations.

Regardless of which party is in the majority, no matter what year you look at, the stories all start having the same familiar ring.

The more things change, the more they stay the same. Until I meandered through the Pulitzer website, I hadn't truly understood that hoary saying.

However, as I scrolled grumpily through each year, clucking endlessly to myself, another major truth became clear. Maybe I can paraphrase it with another ancient saying: There's always a silver lining. Because after all the prizes won for ferreting out corporate and governmental sewage, we get the Pulitzer winners for literary works and music.

I mean, it's a lesson in vision. If you want to stay grumpy, you have that right; but in spite of bad news, there's also good news, lovely news. In 1940, with graft rampant in Connecticut, William Saroyan won for his play, *The Time of Your Life*. The same year the *Chi-*

cago Daily News exposed fraud in the Illinois State Auditor's office, John F. Kennedy won for *Profiles in Courage*. Harper Lee won for *To Kill a Mockingbird*, the same year the *Amarillo Globe Times* shellacked lazy Texas cops. In 1989, when the *Atlanta Journal and Constitution* exposed racial discrimination in Atlanta banks, Anne Tyler won for *Breathing Lessons*.

The poet Robert Frost won the Pulitzer five times, the playwright Thornton Wilder three.

Knowing that these artists—and plenty of others—have fought the good fight against darkness gives me hope. That they've been amply and publicly rewarded for this good fight gives me even more hope.

"Plus ça change, plus c'est la même chose," said Jean-Baptiste Alphonse Karr, a French writer I'd never heard of before I looked him up— "The more it changes, the more it's the same thing." If that's true, then in addition to idiotic governments and criminal corporations, we'll also always have people who create great music, who write to inspire and delight us, who give us elegance and genius—and let us bask in light.

Always.

Dec. 12, 2002

Look for Gold

I N THE AUBURN Library's Beecher Room last Saturday, I chatted briefly with a woman I respect, with whom I've been friendly for years. She's not a happy camper.

As this 80-something woman bemoaned the state of society, humanity, the environment, the economy and politics, I couldn't disagree with her. I often do the same thing, often in this space. Then she said things have never been this bad. It's hopeless, was her implication.

Well. I had two reactions to that.

First, I speculated that when her mother was 80-something, she, too, had probably looked around at the changes wrought since her youth and the problems endemic to society and couldn't believe it either. I said that most likely everyone in every age and in every country looks around and laments the state of the world.

However, I was very aware that we sat in two of at least 50 chairs I had set up, near a table with two 16mm projectors, all ready for that day's Silver Screen Classic Movie presentation. My blood hummed in happy anticipation. In about half an hour I would be happily responsible for happily entertaining a happy group of people.

I'm not so naïve that I think Silver Screen is the solution to this country's myriad problems. No matter how many years I keep doing it, Silver Screen won't cure diabetes or cancer. It won't overturn corrupt administrations or alleviate illiteracy. It won't end poverty, war and injustice.

But it certainly doesn't contribute to them. Instead, it makes me feel good. It makes others feel good. It contributes to the well-being of the community.

All right, enough self-promotion. Besides, I'm just using Silver Screen as an example. You could insert the Auburn Symphony in its place. Or the Art Walk. Or Fast Fridays, the Mandarin Festival, Cruise Night, the summer concerts in the Library Garden Theater and the Festival of Lights parade. Auburn is richer for all these. And that's just the beginning of a very long list.

No matter when or where we live, we'll always find ugliness, especially if we look for it.

So be it. The solution? If you keep finding ugliness, look for something else. Look for gold. Better yet, be the gold. Thumb your nose at corruption and idiocy. Choose honesty and wisdom instead. Be a good person, friend, parent, spouse, citizen. Have a good time.

Regardless of the insane national debt, you can keep yours under control. You can open doors, smile, pick up after yourself, keep your promises, return phone calls, make people laugh. Yes, politicians lie, but that doesn't mean you must. Spite them. Tell the truth.

Although my goal is to avoid repeating myself in this space from one year to the next, it turns out I do. I've written on this topic before—that focusing on the negative blinds you to the positive everywhere around you. And once you start looking, you find it.

If I focused solely on ugliness, only took that part of life seriously, I wouldn't notice when a checker pointed out I gave her $10 when she knew I meant to give her $5. I wouldn't notice when a man in my bank got his wallet back because someone found it and returned it. I wouldn't notice when someone thanked me for holding the door open.

Indeed, if I only focused on the junk, I probably wouldn't have held the door open in the first place.

Continually railing against the bastard machine paralyzes you and convinces you that there's no solution and no hope, that the only reasonable response is pessimism.

If that happens, if you succumb to hopelessness, yours is a self-fulfilling prophecy. You've lost. And the bad guys have won.

Sept. 14, 2008

Civil Disagreements

I GET DRESSED to NPR news at 6:30 A.M. every morning. I hear them talk about the brawls in the Middle East. I hear about deadly confrontations between Pakistan and India, the Shiites and the Sunnis, the Hamas and Israel over the tunnels between the Gaza Strip and Egypt that the Hamas use to smuggle arms and people, and the battle to stop the smuggling and the battle to stop the battle to stop the smuggling.

And that violence is in only one small corner of the world. If I keep listening, I hear about bloodshed in other small corners of the world, battles that have raged for weeks or decades or centuries.

I keep being astonished. And I suppose astonishment is a reasonable response to my astonishment. Heck—if people have always behaved like this, why should I be surprised?

However, I don't drive on ruined streets past smoking rubble. After listening to those daily NPR horror stories, this astonishes me, too.

Every morning I hear about carnage and ghastly behavior, yet every day I see heart-warming evidence that people can control themselves.

This brings me to that cheery bunch that gathers for coffee midmorning at the High Street parking lot next to Rico's Barber Shop and Depoe Bay. You've seen them smoking and laughing and debating and waving their arms. You may even have joined them sometimes. Maybe you're one of them.

Mostly men. Retired guys, working guys, guys taking a break. Some old, some older, some young, some younger. Sometimes I join the group, briefly, just to say hi and hear a joke as I go back to work.

The thing is, their politics vary.

Vary? Hee, hee, what an understatement. Their politics wave at each other from the rim of a chasm so vast it spans time zones. Some guys are liberal, others conservative. As a result, they disagree about nearly every topic you can throw at them, from taxes and global warming to gun control and gay marriage. Each side is convinced it's reasonable and right, and each is convinced the other is unreasonable and wrong.

Yet nobody's ever had to call the cops to break up fistfights. You never see drying pools of blood on the blacktop or body parts littering the gutter after the men go back to work or back home. Any time I approach this group, I never hear yelling or imprecations or implications about one's heritage. I never hear overt threats. Never even hear veiled threats.

It's all very friendly, very civil. It's a joy. It's a joy not only because these guys like each other and get along, but also because I know they're not unique. If these disagreers gather peacefully every day at this spot, I know other disagreers gather peacefully every day at other spots in Auburn.

So this must happen in other spots every day in other towns in other counties and in other states. And it must also happen in other countries. It's the violence that attracts attention.

I like to imagine that, several blocks away from a confrontation in Belfast, a couple of brave Protestants and a couple of brave Catholics might get together for coffee and conversation. Maybe now in Rwanda, a couple of brave Tutsis and a couple of brave Hutus are willing to meet and talk and find the humanity in each other.

Heck. If the group on High Street can do it, everyone can.

In other news: I chatted a few days ago with Jennifer Keck, the executive director for the Symphony. We talked a little about this town and a few of the things that make it wonderful.

I told her how great it is to live here at the same time as the Symphony exists. I share this river of time with great people and organizations in this wonderful town, and it's a kick. How lucky we are.

Even though the morning group on High Street finds a lot to argue about, I know they'd agree with me on that.

April 26, 2009

Be the Change You Wish to See

S EVERAL MONTHS AGO, I talked with a woman I knew in high school. She's as intense now as she was then, as involved and as articulate. Not long into our conversation, I knew I'd write about it.

See, for the past four decades, she's worked for companies that focus on the importance of living green. Recycling. Reusing. Being careful with resources. Reducing. She makes a good living. She found a way to promote what she believes in and lives. She found a need and filled it. Lucky woman.

However, in spite of her work, she sees waste everywhere, sees extravagance, overuse and pollution. She saw smog when she began and she still does.

She feels she's spun her wheels for the past 40 years, wasted her energy, wasted her time, wasted her breath.

I've thought about this conversation often, and I've come to the same conclusions each time.

First, she's wrong, of course. The ideas of recycling, reusing, reducing—they're on people's minds more than they were 40 years ago. Recycling is basic these days. I mean, you recycle, don't you? Of course you do.

Second, she's spent her life doing what she loves. She believes in this. It's her passion, her obsession. It's her reason for being. She couldn't not have done this. I know many people who would envy her.

Finally, rather than grumble about how little difference her efforts have made, she should consider what would have happened if she had turned her back on trying to improve things. If she had gone into fashion design, say. Or advertising.

I know, this is sort of like casting her in *It's a Wonderful Life,* showing her what her community would be like without her. Because we need people's energy in order to make a difference.

What if everyone gave up? What if everyone just figured what's the use, there's nothing to be done, it's hopeless? As Gandhi said, "You may never know what results come of your action, but if you do nothing there will be no result."

"It's important to keep on keeping on," said Millee Livingston, of the Sierra Foothills branch of the Women's International League for Peace and Freedom. She, too, has worked tirelessly for years— urging governments and individuals to seek peaceful ways of communicating and confrontation.

Have her efforts been in vain just because people continue to shoot at each other?

"Change happens slowly," Millee said. Even so, working for that change "is not wasting time. I see evidence that things are changing, and we're making a difference with young people. They're the future."

"I commend her on a life well spent," said Eric Peach, the very vocal and visible representative of PARC, Protect American River Canyons.

He shared good news: At last Saturday's annual American River

Cleanup, "there was a lot less trash" than in previous years.

"But we can't get complacent," he said. "There's always more to do."

Of course this can get discouraging. But "wherever we are now," he said, after the years spent encouraging others to appreciate and protect the river canyons and their beauty and ecology, "even though we haven't made as much an effect as we hoped to, we have made some changes. And we're better people because of our efforts."

There.

The world can always use better people. Better people effect change. They're the ones who make a difference.

April 24, 2010

Learning from a Role Model

I SAW HER at the gym after my workout. For just a second, I considered not greeting her. She hadn't seen me, wouldn't have missed my hello, would have happily gone about her day without realizing I hadn't said anything. And I was so sweaty! I was just a mess! How simple not to subject her to my wet hair, dripping face and aromatic self.

But I have this doctor, see, who is also a friend and a role model. And I thought about him, as I often do. Years ago I'd seen him here, at the same gym, on the other side of the weight room and hadn't greeted him. He was busy with his own effort, and I thought he hadn't seen me.

But later he came up to me and said hi, and we talked about the benefits—to both him and me—of greeting each other. Just a second, just a moment, nothing big, just one person acknowledging another.

Yes, it's only a second. But what if everyone decided to give others a smile and a nod and a hello how are you? Instead of not? What friendliness would result. And how wonderful to be a part of that. Instead of not.

All this went through my head as I passed my friend, who still hadn't seen me. But I got stuck on my memory of that conversation with my doctor, just as if I'd caught my shirt on a nail. And I turned back and said hello. We had a wonderful few minutes catching up. The result of those few minutes? We were both fuller than we'd been before.

James—my doctor—may or may not consider himself a role model. I don't think that's his goal. Instead, I imagine his goal is his well-being as well as others', his joy as well as others', his mental and physical health as well as others'.

He'd be happy, I guess, if others considered him a role model. I know I'm happy to consider him one of mine.

Using James like this—and I am using him—has a startling result. And as I try to think of how to explain it, I recall part of a poem by Walter de la Mare: "It's a very odd thing/As odd can be/That whatever Miss T eats/Turns into Miss T."

So what was once a peach becomes, now that it's part of Miss T, just that—part of Miss T and not a peach anymore.

So if I use the behavior I've learned from James, that behavior becomes mine, a part of me. I might think of it as his, but nobody else does. This is how Susan behaves, and that's all there is to it. And the more I behave this way, the more like myself it feels.

Surely that's a good thing. Of course it is. Even if I think of James as I act more and more like myself.

###

Aug. 19, 2012

two

Men and Women

YEARS BEFORE I started writing And Another Thing, I read a variety of columns by women. Many of these writers went out of their way to smirk at men and roll their eyes at them. How silly they are, they smirked. How ridiculous, how fussy, how fusty. How coarse and hairy.

Most of the time, by "men" they meant "husbands."

How come these women scoffed at their husbands in print? You do that when you don't like somebody. And if you don't like your husband, how come you're married to him? Plus, what does this say about her? "Yeah, I made do with an idiot, and although I'm better than he is, I guess I'll stay put."

So who's the idiot?

I swore I'd never denigrate my husband in print. Why would I? What a coarse and hairy thing to do.

Not everything in this section discusses Don. But it deals with connections and relationships between men and women, and since I'm most familiar with his and my relationship, you'll find his name mentioned here more than once.

Spectacular Men

SICK WITH LONGING, I gazed in misery at my visiting cousin as he loped easily in the yard, playing catch with my brothers. The sun glinted off his wire-rimmed glasses. Overcome, I could not look away from Jack's face, from those blue eyes behind his lenses.

The thought of speaking to him paralyzed me. After all, he was older. He was a man. He was 20.

That steamy night, sleep eluded me. Sleep? With Jack under the same roof, breathing the same air? Finally, restless and thirsty—really, I just wanted a glass of water—I crept from my room. I felt for the hall light switch and turned it on.

I quailed at my recklessness: The light dimly illuminated Jack, asleep on the living room floor, thrust halfway out of his sleeping bag. Oh, my, that fabulous face. Without glasses he looked different, as if someone else lay there. He was two men, and my throat tightened at the sight of both of them.

He stirred in his sleep. I fled. Two faces invaded my tortured fantasies that night.

After years of practice, I'm pleased to report, I can finally speak in complete sentences to attractive men. But put glasses on them? More often than not, I forget to finish those sentences.

Yes, my weakness for men in glasses endures. My first boyfriend, a sweet boy with a car and just a few pimples, swore his undying love while tortoise-shell frames dignified his face.

Although few leading men wear glasses, how can we overlook Harold Lloyd and Groucho Marx? They don't exude raw sexuality, exactly, but an aura of humor and intelligence does surround them. But then there's William Hurt and Kevin Costner, both of whom I've had the enviable opportunity of seeing in glasses.

I'm not the only one enchanted by a man in horn rims. In the 1956 comedy *Some Like It Hot,* Tony Curtis seduces Marilyn Monroe by slipping *into* a pair of glasses. It works. *She* knows.

But since that movie appeared, and since that painful summer with my cousin, I have witnessed an insidious trend. Lately, too many men opt for contact lenses.

Don't snow me with the excuses of convenience and accurate vision. I understand what's really behind this scheme: a prejudice against men who wear glasses. Boys still subject each other to the derisive "four eyes!" insult.

Worse, the image lingers of the fussy banker, holding the fate of your loan application in his hands as he squints at you over his pince-nez.

Men with prescription lenses suffer the undeserved, inaccurate reputation of being sissies and weaklings.

I suppose I can't blame anyone for deciding on contact lenses to avoid those unfair stereotypes.

But I won't stop any shortsighted women from leaping at the hunks with 20-20 vision and frameless profiles. That just leaves me with the rest, all those men with a second face to discover.

See, when I meet a man in glasses, I grow accustomed to his

face, those eyes framed behind those lenses. But another layer lurks, and I know it. Finally comes the moment of unveiling: a new man. Not better, just… new. And the woman who unites with such a gem? She has the luxury of loving two faces.

But I worry that all these bespectacled—spectacular—men, unaware of their subtle attraction, will opt to sacrifice their tantalizing frames for the blandness of contacts. What a mistake, surrendering such a distinction in favor of the conformity of one predictable face.

And what a mistake to withhold the luxury of two faces from any woman who might happen to love you.

You know I'm right. After all, which do you find more enticing: monotony, or mystery?

I don't have to think twice. Give me, give me what I cry for: Give me the man with glasses.

Nov. 29, 1987

FYI: If you've met Don, you'll note he wears glasses. That's not just because he's now a senior citizen. He's always worn glasses. Hee, hee, hee.

Midnight Hour Physics

T HE HOUR—SOMETIME after midnight, way, way past our bedtime—of course contributed to my inability to understand the concept of what he said. I deserved this extensive conversation, though. I kept asking questions. After all, it's one of my jobs as a wife, as it's one of his as a husband, to be an ear.

And what my ear heard, after he regaled me with the exciting story of how his team won the softball game, was that the top of a curveball moves faster than the bottom. Because, his reasoning went, the top's always ahead of the bottom.

Don't get me wrong. We don't often have discussions about physics. I think it's the first we've endured in our 15 years together. At the very least, it's the first one we've endured when we should have been asleep.

No, I argued, yawning. Regardless of how many physics classes he's taken, he couldn't tell me that the top of a ball travels faster than the bottom.

This isn't to say he didn't try. First he gave me all this guff about the direction of the air relative to the ball; then some junk about the top of the ball moving faster relative to the air. And when that didn't work, he had the nerve to bring up "Bernoulli's equation and all, you know?"

Oh, sure. *That* old trick.

And he tried several times to convince me, first by insisting that he knew better than I because mine had been one of those—ick— liberal arts educations, and second by demonstrating his cockeyed theory to me, using an old Santana album cover as a visual aid.

Look, he said, turning the cardboard over in his hands as he paced across the living room. See where this point is, compared to this point? Well, yes, I saw, but the whole cover moved too. Was he trying to tell me that an object is really only its molecules? And since some molecules get to where they're going before others because they're at the back of the train, the first molecules travel faster than the second group? Eek.

He winced. I'd missed his point (no surprise). The poor guy was astonished that I wouldn't believe him—nor could I recognize the obvious.

It was equally obvious to me that he was mistaken. What he said wasn't logical.

It was also obvious that he believed what he said because people he'd trusted, people he'd considered authorities, had told him the same thing.

He couldn't have come to this conclusion on his own, I said. Someone early on had to tell him. And he would have to just believe it, to take a leap of faith. Because it made no sense.

He believed it was true, then, because he believed it. I didn't believe it because I didn't believe it. I couldn't make that leap of faith, accept the evidence of things unseen.

Physics, it seemed to me through my haze of tiredness, resembled Zen or Scientology, Christianity or Judaism. You don't come to believe the tenets of those faiths all by yourself. It takes other people, others you trust, to turn you on to one religion or another, to help you make that leap of faith.

The two of us in the living room being amazed at one another's inability to see could have been a Methodist and a Navajo, a Taoist and an Orthodox Jew, a Catholic and a Buddhist. A Republican and a Democrat.

Sure of our beliefs, both of us were positive that if the other would just leap, say *yes, you're right, yes, I see and it's wonderful*—well, the world would be a better place.

Certainly we'd have a more peaceful house.

As I remember, we finally got to bed. But he never convinced me, really, although I must—I always must—defer to his superior knowledge of and his vast experience with physics.

If not physics, then certainly baseball.

May 3, 1991

Uppity Woman's Punishment

H E *SAID* HE married me because he liked my sensitivity, my sense of humor and my... hmm. I know somewhere in there he mentioned my intelligence. He said it more than once, though not—as I think about it—in front of witnesses.

I've noticed a problem, however. Maybe he's like some of these men threatened by a woman's intelligence. I've heard of them, even met a few, but I never suspected that he'd belong to that camp. Heck—he's a smart guy, and he knows I know it. He can't need to demonstrate his superiority or put me in my place.

It must be that, though. Otherwise, why would he send me to the hardware store alone?

Sure, he always draws me a picture of what he wants, scrawled meticulously on the back of an old telephone bill. I always go off armed with specific measurements. And each time, innocently, I say sure, yes, I'll go. How much trouble could I have?

Lordy, it's awful. He'll remain back at the house, peacefully chained to a major appliance, like the washing machine—or some part of the house, like the bathroom or attic. But I stand forsaken in one of innumerable identical aisles crammed with innumerable maddening identical pieces of metal.

Look at all this stuff: molly screws, wood screws, sheet metal screws, panhead screws, bolts, nuts, washers, brads, and nails. And each is of a different length and thickness: no. 8 by 3/8ths of an inch, no. 6 by 5/8ths of an inch, 1/4 inch by 9/10ths of an inch, or 3/4ths of an inch, or 9/16ths of an inch. And my choices don't end there, because screws boast different pitches *(pitches,* for God's sake) and types of threads: metric, American and Wentworth.

Whoever he was.

Those clerks must be in on it with him. He probably phones them and gives them precise instructions on what to say to me. They'll take his elaborate drawing, scowl at it and laugh at me. *Lady,* they'll smirk. I grit my teeth. Nobody else calls me *Lady* like that. Then they ask me these impossible questions: *What's this for, why does he need this, why'd he ask for this 5/8ths of an inch screw when a 3/4ths would do just fine?* If I had the vocabulary to answer them, they'd never ask me. If I *knew,* they'd never ask me.

Arrgh.

When he really wants to put me in my place he forces me to deal with car parts. Me, a person who can't believe that a hairline crack in a brake shoe, a cylinder, a piston or a valve can possibly be as big a deal as he makes it out to be.

He called one night from Marysville, stuck and in trouble. "Do me a favor," he said. "Go in the garage and bring me my ratchet, my socket set, my valve gauge, my voltmeter—"

I feverishly scribbled out a nearly indecipherable and badly misspelled list of items. He went on and on, and not one thing sounded familiar.

Things got worse when I hunted around in the garage. Because he knows me, he'd described everything in vivid detail. But the rubber hose had no shiny silver handle and the black plastic hammer-like tool wasn't calibrated in inches.

I piled everything in the truck except the newspapers and the dog food dish. In my haste I nearly threw in the lawn mower. Who knows? Maybe he could've used it.

Of course I felt like a dope, especially when he pulled out one obscure piece of metal and with a sigh of immense satisfaction (he never sighs that way with me) climbed under the hood with it. I'll bet there wasn't really anything wrong with the engine. He probably had an hour to kill and just figured he needed to bring me down a notch.

It's been a while since he's punished me this way. I have to watch myself, though. Otherwise he'll think up some flimsy excuse— oh, like the toilet exploding—to send me to the hardware store again.

June 7, 1991

James Brown's Scream

THE WOMAN BURST through the door of the restaurant—empty except for me, the only customer, and the waitress, her friend—with a beatific smile and hands that wouldn't stop fluttering.

"He came over last night," she burbled as the waitress poured my coffee and I listened. "I was a mess but he didn't seem to care. And he said he'd call me this afternoon and we'd do something."

Dancing a little, her eyes rolling to the ceiling, she added that he'd met her daughter—a toddler, I assumed, since she was pretty young herself—and liked her, and didn't mind that she had a child.

"I'll call you later," she giggled as she moved to the door, her face still beaming, and she left.

We watched her go. I looked at the waitress. "Is she in love?" I asked, unnecessarily.

"Uh-huh," she said, also unnecessarily.

Watching as the besotted woman drifted across the street, oblivious to the cars approaching her, I envied her, remembering those first buzzing, heady, breathless, astonishing, single-minded, melancholy, painful, sweet, fanatical days of falling in love with the man I married.

I've done a little research—falling in love apparently affects men differently than it does women. Upon first falling in love, most men don't go mooning around, don't keep intricate track of how often eyes meet or hands touch. Men don't make an extensive record of what she said when he said this. Men don't agonize the way women do, don't wonder whether to keep a handle on themselves or let themselves go and make it clear how they feel about her.

Of course, there are always exceptions, but mostly just women go off the deep end. That woman in the restaurant has, and her falling in love is my falling in love. Each time I fell in love it was the same. It happened the last time in 1978, a Saturday in September at the Monterey Jazz Festival. I was a mess for weeks afterward.

I felt as if all my nerve ends were on alert, as if my skin were James Brown's trademark shout personified. Yes, I carried on conversations with other people, even drove my Volkswagen as if I were in my right mind—but my whole being cared only about seeing him, and I looked for him wherever I went.

It really was wonderful, in a wretched sort of way.

Wretched? Oh, of course. You can't live like that, tripping over yourself in parking lots. You can't get anything done, really, with all those hormones spurting through you.

Luckily, this first goofy, heady, spine-tingling part lasts only until you know each other well enough to fight. Then you either get to know each other better or you become the subject of a country-western song.

If you're lucky, what comes after that reckless, combustible stage is less reckless and combustible, less like pitching and rolling on the open sea.

If you're lucky, what comes after this stage is great friendship, intense loyalty, a rich, golden wheat field full of nourishment; a net to fall in; the reverberations of the beats of a kettle drum, reverberations so intense they resonate through the floorboards and assail your feet as you feel them in the air surrounding you and they invade your innards and vibrate there.

But there's nothing *fun* about any of that, nothing tumultuous or dramatic. You don't see "electrifying" or "reckless" in the definitions of friendship or loyalty. Besides, nothing—*nothing*—matches the sensation of adrenaline charging through you, rendering you giddy and unsteady.

So I envied that woman madly in love, helpless in that combustible stage, pitching and rolling on the open sea. I wished her luck, remembering those turbulent weeks of James Brown screaming on my skin.

Briefly. Then I went home and laughed with my husband.

###

Feb. 21, 1992

Loving a Middle-Aged Man

I HEARD HIM yell from the other end of the house. Although sometimes he hollers and has only dropped a screw, something brought me running. He stood wincing with his hand under the faucet, the large vegetable knife on the counter.

"Pretty deep," he muttered as he galloped to the bathroom. I got a towel and the bandages ready and asked if he wanted to go to the emergency room.

"Nope."

"You sure? If it's pretty deep—"

"Nope."

It was just a cut. My reaction was beyond what it should have been. Tears and shaking hands? Just for a cut thumb? Heck, he's cut himself before. But these days, seems he always has something wrong with him: pulled muscles, sore shoulder, bad knees, bad ear.

And then he comes home gloomy and dejected from a semi-pro baseball game. For years, baseball and softball have been his life. Watching those players only reminded him that he can't do what they do. Once he could, but now he can't. And he wants to, more than almost anything.

He wants to race back on a fly ball and know he'll catch it, and fire the ball back to first, off-balance and running the wrong way. He wants to have a perfect eye and strong arms and legs so he can swat the ball through the infield and get on each time. He wants to slide—aches to slide, begs to slide—smoothly into second and poprightup.

He wants to do all these things well, and he watches his body not doing them and it's tough. It's tough for me, too. Because I love him, I want him to be happy. Happy, do you hear? Not disappointed or discouraged.

See, I'm married to a middle-aged man. The night he cut himself I suddenly recognized that every ache and pain I watch him endure is my preparation for the big one: heart attack or cancer or stroke. Every ache is a reminder that he's mortal. Someday I'll have to watch him really hurt, or even—surprise of surprises—he'll have to watch me really hurt.

Someday one will have to watch the other die.

Once, sitting with his back to me on the other side of the bed, unable to look at me, he said he couldn't decide which would be worse, being the one to leave or the one left behind.

I remember the moment he told me cancer and heart disease ran in his family. *Should I leave him now,* I thought, *and avoid the heartbreak I know is coming?* But by that time I was stuck. Now I'm in even further. I couldn't leave if I wanted to. And the longer I stay, the sweeter things become: mellower and funnier and richer.

When I was younger, I got the message that you loved your spouse more the longer you were together. From that I assumed that there was something intentional about it, that on purpose you loved that person more. My callow vision involved, oh, maybe a heart growing bigger as you poured all that love into it.

On this side of that vision, though, I see something far more complex. Maybe a softball, one that has morphed into a dense ball of string. The same size, perhaps even the same weight, this ball of string is more involved, more complicated than that softball.

It's like an embryo. For a long time as those cells divide, the size of the egg stays the same. One cell to two to four to eight to 16 to 32 to 64 and on and on, while still filling the same space. It makes no sense, it's impossible, but there you are.

That's my metaphor. An older love is more complex than a younger one, while filling the same container. I don't necessarily love him more than before, I love him better, differently. The longer we're together the sweeter the relationship. The dearer he becomes, because time keeps passing.

I won't always have him. That means more to me now than it used to.

July 30, 1992

Typical? Really?

I T HAPPENED AGAIN: A woman, fussing at her husband, looked at me and rolled her eyes. "Typical male," she sighed, loud enough for him to hear.

What was he doing that she thought warranted her scornful tone of voice? As far as I could tell, he was hesitating over a pair of shoes—did he want them, did he not, did they fit or didn't they. She said if you're not sure, it's silly to get them. Finally, after a moment of vacillating, he tossed the shoes indifferently into the box and said he'd buy them.

I can't figure out which of these actions is typical of men. Maybe she's convinced that all men buy things they don't want, or that they all vacillate in the shoe store. Maybe she thinks they all figure out what their wives want them to do and do the opposite, just to tweak them. It could also be she thought he was being stupid—and figures stupidity is a typical male attribute.

Don, at that moment, was also vacillating in the shoe store, but he doesn't typically vacillate in shoe stores. Nor is he likely to buy something he doesn't want. And he doesn't spend much time figuring out what I want so he can go strutting off and do the opposite. He ain't stupid, either. Typical.

"Typical male." I hate moments like that. I'm expected to laugh and nod, agree with the speaker, shake my head and be the good ol' girl and go along with the denigration—not only of the dope she thinks she's connected with, but by extension all men. *Isn't that just like a man, they're all alike, can't live with 'em, can't live without 'em, what're you gonna do?*

Feh. I'll volunteer for a root canal before I'll give credence to shabby bigotry like that. And blanket scorn like that is bigotry, even though it's directed at men.

These man-bashers—what do they say?

"Men are so selfish." Selfish? Does this mean they want a good car and a nice house and more money and someone who will wait on them hand and foot? Oh, come on. I want those things. Doesn't everybody?

"Men are such babies when they're sick." I don't feel all that grown up when I have a fever, either.

"They want everything their own way." I do, too.

"Men are always looking." So am I—and for a similar reason. No harm in looking at that lean, tanned racquetball player leaping for the shot. How easy on the eyes.

In general, yes, men are the power brokers. Yes, in general they earn more money than women. In most cases, yes, they're stronger than women. And periodically there's a Packwood or a Tyson who shoves his weight around, making life impossible for women.

That doesn't mean it's OK to denigrate them all. Just as I bristle when I hear disparaging comments about women, I bristle when people badmouth men. Because if it's not OK to ridicule one sex, it's not OK to ridicule the other.

If you do, you have no room to complain when you hear "Ain't that just like a woman?" or "Typical female."

The thing is, I only hear "Isn't that just like a man?" or "Typical male" when he does something she doesn't like. I would bet that no man has ever heard one of those "typical male" comments after he does something sweet, like bringing her ginger ale when her stomach's upset; or loving, like bragging on her accomplishments to his friends; or courteous, like giving up his seat in a crowded bus; or competent, like replacing the garbage disposal.

Why wouldn't you label this behavior typical? I know at least one man for whom these actions are typical, yet there's nothing offensive or annoying about them. And since it's typical, I think his wife's pretty smart for hooking up with him.

I think I'll start a revolution to counteract that bigoted "just like a man" complaint. I'll say it when a man—typically—treats me with respect. .

As for that woman in the shoe store? If she believes that typical male behavior involves boorishness or stupidity, if she believes it's "just like a man" to hurt women or demand the unreasonable, what the hell's she doing married? It just doesn't compute.

###

Aug. 3, 1995

The Census and the Human Race

I FINALLY MAILED in my census form. Late. And it wasn't even the long form, that fascinating-sounding thing most people didn't get. No, we got the short form, a picayune disappointment that just asked about what kind of a place I live in, my age, sex, and race. It was so short that I completed most of it several weeks ago.

I just had questions seven and eight left for my husband, the ones concerning race. I had to wait for him to answer them. I couldn't answer them on my own.

What? Yes, I see you rolling your eyes at me. Come now, Susan, don't you know Don's race?

Yes. Yes, I know his race. Pardon my testiness. It's just that whenever any question regarding race comes up, I can't predict his response. And I knew from long years of experience and conversation that it would be absurd to second-guess him.

So I had him do it, and it took him a while to decide what to say. That's why I just mailed it yesterday. Your honor.

I think part of him considers any race question pointless. What difference does it make? Why does it matter? Why should it matter?

And, forced as I am to think about it, married to him, nowadays it takes me longer to consider my race when the subject comes up. Although not as long as it takes Don.

On the form, for example, in question eight, I saw white, all by itself. After that came black, African American or Negro. OK.

Next came American Indian. I agree, we need to count members of all the tribes, from the Choctaws and Powhatans to the Apaches and Cherokees and Maidus. Yes, we should count everybody. But I want to see the anthropological evidence that American Indian is a separate race.

Then it got even more absurd. Chinese was separate from Japanese. Vietnamese was separate from Korean. Is Korean a race? Is it a separate race from Filipino?

If they do this to Asians, why don't they do it to Africans? Why not inquire if you're Rwandan or Egyptian, Sudanese or Moroccan? What if your ancestors came from Chad or Mali?

And what about whites? Why not insist that Canadian is a separate race from Hungarian and both are separate from Lithuanians and the Danes? Or, if you really want to start an argument, South Africans.

It's my conjecture that the census people cared less about race than they did ethnic heritage. OK, fine. So why didn't they say so, instead of implying that suddenly we have more than three races?

I have other issues, too. All the ads encouraging us to fill out the census form disparaged any fears we might have about sharing this private information with the government. Don't worry, they said, "Your answers are protected by law." The law says nobody else can look at the information you gave the census department.

Yeah, so it's the law—now. So what? Used to be the law women couldn't vote. Once you couldn't sell booze. Yes, yes, yes, it took 13 years to change back that last one, but even so. Nothing says the law can't change. Changes all the time. So it's ridiculous to inundate us with reassurances that no-o-body else will ever see the incredibly valuable stuff we tell the census people.

Plus, I figure, with all our private data on every government computer you can think of, they really don't need us to send all this information them. Probably they just want it for corroboration.

I imagine they already knew, for example, what Don would put down for question number eight. They just wanted to make sure. Actually, he fooled me. Because his great-great-grandparents came here from Chile, sometimes says he's of Latino heritage.

Sometimes he checks Other as his race, and puts Other in the blank that asks for elaboration. I figure that's why the house creaks at night, and the reason for the phone calls that say they're wrong numbers.

This time, he checked "Some Other Race" and put American in the blanks underneath. I didn't do that. I said I was white. But I don't blame him. If you can check Samoan or Guamanian as your race, it seems perfectly legitimate—and consistent—to put American.

Besides. He answered the question. It asked him "to indicate what this person considers himself to be." Don considers himself an American. I guess that settles it.

###

April 13, 2000

Public or Private Involvement

I BELONG TO a monthly play-reading group. We get 10 copies of a play and we sit around and read it to each other. About a year ago, we read one whose name I don't remember, but I think it became the musical *1776*. The playwright formed a drama around the letters that John and Abigail Adams had written to each other.

John Adams, our second president, was involved in the Continental Congress, helped form the basis of the United States, hammered out the rights we eventually came away with. He contributed to the vital business of forming a country. He put his considerable energy toward the revolutionary ideas that all men are created equal, and that we have the unalienable rights of life, liberty, and the pursuit of happiness.

What thrilling ideas. He helped craft them. He presided at the birth of this country.

This great man was also a husband and father, with a family back in Massachusetts. He helped carve a nation; Abigail raised the children. He made stunning speeches; she contributed to daily life in Quincy. He debated the concept of freedom; she gave birth without him. He went to France; she went to bed alone. He knew he was making history; she nursed a son through scarlet fever.

Again and again, they separated for months at a time.

Her life was basic and modest, the life of a housewife left at home. She'd married for love, for companionship. And while she encouraged his participation in politics, she must have sighed a lot. She saw the full moon by herself. She was alone when she looked out the back window and saw the sun casting low shadows in the late afternoon light. The fruit trees in the back yard bloomed without him. Someone else had to shovel the snow.

She loved him. She wanted him to be part of the business of making a country, making a name for himself. What could be more important than that?

Yet because she loved him, she wanted him with her. What a tough choice, what selfish, *mememe* thoughts: *I married you, I want you with me, I want you next to me. The heck with the big picture, sit here with me and watch the sunset while I feel your warmth along my side. Forget those pesky responsibilities. Make love to me, damn it.*

When the group of us—all married women, all middle-aged—discussed the play, we recognized the searing dilemma the two found themselves in.

And as I write this, I get teary, because it's a terrible quandary. Intelligent people have to be involved in moving the country, making a difference. Someone has to do it. Someone—someone smarter than the rest of us—has to dedicate the time and energy and passion to sit in the meetings, agitate, argue, convince, lobby, push.

At the same time—and this is what brings tears to my eyes—can you sacrifice the humble, lovely moments (and months and years) of being with the person you love? You married that person for a reason, after all.

How wonderful to be able to share something you're reading

with your spouse, or laugh at private jokes, or see your daughter's first steps together. Or celebrate an anniversary or a birthday together, year after year. Or eat dinner together, night after night for years. Or watch the moon rise, or gasp together at a shooting star. These feel so good.

These bits make up the life of a family, stitch the fabric of your life together. They're vital to a partnership.

But they're private. And as large as they feel, they're small in the scheme of things, small in comparison with creating a country, or making it better.

Forget the terrible quandary—it's a terrible choice for anyone to have to make. And while I respect the people who choose—and chose—to make our country and make it better in that big way, I don't envy them. I'm too selfish. I don't want to do that. But I'm glad they do.

Jan. 10, 2002

Mundane Marriage a Hot Topic

W HEN I WAS a graduate student at Chico State, the group I hung out included Sandy, Dick and Patty. Dear friends Patty and Sandy had known each other forever. Sandy and Dick were married.

But when they married, they'd made an agreement: Sandy saw no reason to change anything about her friendship with Patty. Patty was part of the deal. So the three of them lived together. And you knew that whenever you saw one, you'd see the other two.

There was no implication of sexuality among them. They were just a threesome. Nor was there any sense of three being a crowd. Dick understood the situation and went into the marriage with his eyes open. Patty understood, too.

I think often of that trio, most recently with the furor about marriage in the media, in Massachusetts, Washington and San Francisco. Because that furor centers on one man and one woman, married, living in the same house with their children.

But we all know there are variations to this picture. That college threesome, for example. And my husband Don and me. Yes, we've been married for decades, but we decided almost immediately not to have children.

I know others who have similarly unconventional marriages. Unconventional to me, anyway. I know two married couples who live apart, in separate homes in different towns. They see each other on the weekends, or they make dates. I couldn't do that. For one thing, I couldn't afford it. I have other reasons, but they're too personal to tell you.

And I know of other couples in love who have chosen not to marry. This is nothing new. We all know people like this, and most of them live together. But these couples don't even do that. Instead, they've just been connected since dirt was invented.

Last week I talked about living under the radar. This, too, is living under the radar. Yes, most people marry and live in the same house; yes, the majority of couples have children, but so what?

Last summer I had this cool idea: I'd approach those people I knew who had marriages or relationships different from the norm and we'd talk about them, and I'd discuss them here. I thought that would be interesting. I thought it would make a good column.

Hey look, I planned to say, *all of you who insist you know what marriage is and what it looks like. Here are people who live life differently from you and are still happy.*

So I've thought about this a while. But suddenly, the subject of marriage has roiled into something touchy, political, prickly. It's astonishing. Who'd a' thunk it?

I've always considered marriage the white bread and foxtrot of relationships. There's no topic in the world more conservative, innocuous or banal than marriage.

But now it's a polarizing issue. It's no longer innocuous or banal. As a result, no one within those unconventional relationships will talk to me.

Well, actually, I imagine they'd all be tickled to talk to me about their relationships. But they don't want to be quoted or identified.

It's nothing personal, they say.

But it is. It couldn't be more personal. Mind you, they aren't ashamed. They aren't embarrassed. They just don't want anyone peeking in at them, figuratively or any other way. They figure how they choose to live and love is, in the end, none of my business.

And because it's none of my business, it's none of your business, either. It can't possibly make any difference to you or your marriage how these people have molded their marriages and relationships to suit themselves. Can't possibly make any difference to the government either.

Shoot. I wanted this to be a different column. And it might have been, in a different political climate. Marriage, a hot potato? I still think it's the oddest thing.

###

March 18, 2004

three

Rufus T. Firefly

R UFUS T. FIREFLY *began as Groucho's character in the Marx Brothers' best movie,* Duck Soup, *from 1933. President of Freedonia, he lusts after Margaret Dumont—well, at least he lusts after her money. For some reason, he declares war on neighboring Sylvania, and all hell breaks loose. This screwy comedy stars four screwballs, and old Rufus is the screwiest of them all.*

Therefore.

I know, I know, Rufus is a man's name. That's been pointed out to me more than once. But my Rufus is crazy. So yes, she has a man's name, but that just means she has a man's name. Proves she's crazy. Or something.

I feel I must clarify: Rufus is fictional. I have never left my bed to meet anyone at Auburn's Clock Tower in the middle of the night. I stress this because people have approached Don, wondering, "Does she really...?"

No.

Clear Proof of a Conspiracy

S HE CALLS HERSELF Rufus T. Firefly. Soon after the Oklahoma City explosion and the headlines about citizen militias, black helicopters and United Nations conspiracies, I started getting cryptic phone calls from her.

"Think that's all there is to it, Rushton?" she'd hiss at me. "A bunch of crackpot men playing soldier in the woods? If you think that's all there is to it, you deserve what you get! Pa-a-ahhh!"

At first I shrugged her off. She seemed like such a weirdo. Plus, I figure if there's really a conspiracy, I can't do much about it. I'm not clever when it comes to intrigue—give me a Robert Ludlum book and I'm lost after the first three pages.

The worst part, though? Rufus insisted on meeting me in the middle of the night. I sleep in the middle of the night. I admit it. I'm not proud.

But she blew up when she heard my excuse. "Sure," she hollered. "Sleep, Rushton. Let others stand guard on your freedom while you lie in bed! The price of freedom is eternal viligance!"

"You mean vigilance," I corrected her, and she started screaming again. I could only shut her up by agreeing to meet her on Tuesday at 2:30 A.M. at the Clock Tower on Lincoln Way.

I heard her before I saw her, muttering about the IRS, the General Assembly and the Security Council. When I reached the bricks, she quieted, and gathered to her all the cans, newspapers and pamphlets she had piled next to her on the bench.

"Rushton?"

"The blood will run when the panther strikes," I said.

"You think you're so funny," Rufus grumbled. "Wait till you're hanging by your thumbs in an empty warehouse at DeWitt because the United Nations has repealed the Second Amendment."

Quickly, she elaborated on the United Nations conspiracy. It's a snare, she insisted, intended to destroy all individual freedom for all freedom-loving Americans.

"Look," she said, brandishing one of the pamphlets in her lap. It was the United Nations Charter. "If you take the first letter of every fifth word in the preamble, you get TSSIU THAPOO AW-TAL TBLELOA TSTTAUI FEACT GTWPG AODOT.

"They want you to think that's nonsense. But it's really in code. When you decipher it, you get this treasonous message: 'Death to all Christian nations. Gun control cures cancer. Mandatory helmet laws. I buried Paul.'"

I must have looked skeptical, because she held up her hand to keep me quiet. "And you know who's behind this? Atheists, of course. And homosexuals, Communists, feminists, Hillary Clinton, the media and the ACLU. Look at that, 'Death to all Christian nations'!" She jabbed at the paper. "Comes as no surprise to me. All atheists are communists, because communists don't believe in God, either—so none of 'em have any morals."

I yawned, and thought of Don at home in bed. Lucky guy. *"All* atheists? *All* homosexuals? *All—"*

"Still don't believe me?" she snarled. "Well, this'll convince you. You know those stickers on the backs of highway signs, directing United Nations troops when they invade?" I shook my head.

"The plot's far more complex than that, Rushton. Look here!" She held out cans of soup and cola, cracker boxes and even dollar bills. On each were indiscriminate letters and numbers, some immediately visible, like the serial numbers on the bills. Others took really looking for, like those stamped on the ends of the cans.

Rufus elaborated on the mystery of these symbols. "They're part of the conspiracy, too. Each is a message to the United Nations troops." She held up a can of Contadina tomato sauce. In the glow of the stoplight I could just make out 5054AC1A081 and then 08:00.

"That one's simple," she said with a grim smile. "Kidnap Rush Limbaugh at 8 A.M. on election day in 1996." Then she frowned. "Unless," she added, "instead of zeros, those are actually the letter O. If that's the case, it says 'Kurt Cobain died for your sins.'"

I was staggered. If Rufus is right, evidence of an impending invasion is everywhere. The more I look, the more I find. I used to think those people were nuts.

June 29, 1995

FYI: This was Rufus' first appearance. As we got to know each other better, I got feistier. So did she.

Everything Offends Rufus

S O I DRAGGED myself out in the middle of the night to meet with Rufus again. She kept insisting that the fate of the free world lay in the balance, that liberals were out to slash my rights. She wore me down. I said all right.

As I approached the Clock Tower on Lincoln Way, I didn't see her. But on one of the benches, I saw a box overflowing with magazine ads, bumper stickers and newspaper clippings on the Baptists' boycott of Disney products and the recent court reversal of the Communications Decency Act.

Then I jumped. Iron smashed against metal and reverberated in the darkness. Then again, and again. My ears ringing, I edged down the sidewalk in the direction of the racket. I saw her, wielding a sledgehammer against the bumper of a ten-year-old Chevy. Finally, out of breath, she stopped. I approached her.

"The blood will run when the panther strikes," I said, and peered at the wreckage: twisted chrome and a bumper sticker, now scraped and torn, barely legible. I could just make out the words: *Don' ike m drivi Call 1-800-EAT-S—*

"What—" I began.

She pointed at the bumper sticker. "I suppose you're like all the rest of those namby-pamby mushmouthed liberals who think you can say anything you want and get away with it," she snarled. "I'll bet you don't care if people get offended. Well, there are some of us that do, Rushton, and we're doing something about it."

"So you're planning to take a sledgehammer to everything that offends you? Even people?"

"What a wimp, Rushton," she growled. "You're just going to sit there and take it without ever fighting back, aren't you? If you're a real American, a decent citizen, this junk offends you. It's offensive, and you have the right not to be offended!"

"You may be right," I said. "I'm offended by your banging on this guy's car just because you don't like his bumper sticker."

"What else am I gonna do?" she sneered. "Let him flaunt his odious message? Not me. This way he'll think before he offends somebody again. Extremism in the defense of liberty is no vice."

"You don't have to pay attention. Besides, what about freedom of speech? He has that right."

"What about my rights, Rushton? I'm more important than he is. My values are more important than his stupid bumper sticker. After all, it's not my fault if he's offending me. I don't want to see this, so I shouldn't have to. I'm going to see to it that nobody does."

"Is it that easy, though?" I asked. "How do we decide what's offensive? Who's going to judge?"

"Me!! If I'm offended, it's offensive. End of discussion. Look at this," she said, shoving a stack of bumper stickers in my face: "Happiness is Being Italian."

"We've forced this slimy company into bankruptcy. The message is offensive to everyone who isn't Italian. It's also offensive to the mentally ill, to women with postnatal depression and all those who are dying, because it assumes that all their problems would be solved if they were Italian." Her voice rose. "Now don't tell me you don't find that offensive."

I started to speak but she cut me off. "I know, you think this is too insignificant to worry about. Wrong! We can't let anything slip by. You may think it's harmless, but you see what it can lead to—" She pointed over to the car whose bumper she had demolished. "Trash like that. And trash like you find on the Internet, on TV, in books and movies—and in junk like this." She brandished a newspaper open to a women's underwear ad.

"How dare they print this where children can see it," she hollered. "Plus, it's offensive to women who will never have a body like this."

"It sounds like you think everything's offensive," I said. She shrugged. "But what if I think I should decide for myself?"

"You aren't capable of deciding for yourself," she snarled. "If we think you shouldn't see something, then you shouldn't see it. No right-thinking, patriotic American would want to see it, anyway."

"But what if I think offensiveness is in the eye of the beholder?"

She scowled. "Talk about offensive." She turned and stalked back to that ten-year-old Chevy.

June 20, 1996

Eroding Rights of the Individual

I SHOULD'VE PRETENDED I wasn't home and let the answering machine screen the call. But once again Rufus T. Firefly caught me off guard, startling me out of a deep sleep. I just automatically reached over and picked up the phone. The minute I heard her voice I knew I was doomed.

"Another plot? Can't you just rant at me over the phone?"

"Over the phone?" she ranted. "This is too important to tell you over the phone, Rushton."

She threatened to come to my house if I didn't meet her at the Clock Tower. I had no interest in a paranoid woman showing up on my doorstep, so I pulled on my jeans and heavy socks and went.

She tensed as I approached. She lifted her head.

"The blood will run when the panther strikes," I said, and collapsed onto the bench beside her.

"When will you learn that the erosion of our rights is no laughing matter?" she growled. "You'll regret your laughter when the one-worlders and the imperialist oligarchy have stripped you of your rights. The price of freedom is eternal viligance."

"You mean vigilance," I sighed, and slid away down the bench to avoid her flying spittle as she sputtered in her irritation.

Just as she started to form real words again, I interrupted her. "As much as I enjoy our little chats," I said, crossing my fingers, "I'd like to get back home. What do you want?"

In spite of her red face, she spoke calmly, digging through the overflowing box at her feet.

"It's just one more sorry example of the eroding rights of the individual," she said, waving clippings about Ken Carter, basketball coach of the Richmond High School Oilers. He had benched the team because 15 of the 45 players had chosen to ignore the academic contract they had signed before the season.

"So what if their GPA dropped below 2.3? So what if they came late to class, didn't turn in homework assignments, broke their agreement to sit in front of the classroom? Tell me this, Rushton—what's all this junk got to do with basketball?"

"Nothing," I admitted.

"Right, Rushton, nothing. All that coach needs to care about is how they play basketball, and their record is 13 wins and no losses. If they don't care how they do in class, that's their business. It's up to them, not him. This is just another example of the fascist face of do-gooders in the society—"

I grabbed the fist waving the story in my face. "I hear that they all signed this agreement to come to class on time, keep up their grades, hand in their homework. They agreed to those conditions in order to play basketball. They understood what they were signing. He wasn't asking a heck of a lot. Besides, they broke their agreement."

"So what?" Rufus screeched. She kicked the box. It skittered away and overturned, strewing the bricks with news clippings. "Just because I say I will, does that mean I have to? Nobody else in this country has the obligation to abide by contracts they sign."

"From what I gather," I said, "they brought their grades back up. The coach has unlocked the gym, and they can play their games again. The students recognize that if they want to play basketball, they have to abide by the agreement they made. What's wrong with that?"

She winced and slapped her forehead. "You're as brainwashed as those pathetic 16-year-old stooges. The saps—they just knuckled under. Can't you see, Rushton? Nothing is more important than your individuality, and if some bogus contract turns out to impinge on one's individuality, then you have a right—no, an obligation—to violate that contract. People break agreements all the time and nobody thinks a thing about it. I can't see why you're not outraged."

"Oh, I'm outraged, all right," I said, and continued in spite of her wide-eyed astonishment. "You saw where the story ran on the *Today* Show, *Good Morning America,* CNN and in *People Magazine.* In this country right now, someone who insists on maintaining high standards is an oddball worthy of nationwide coverage. That's what ticks me off, Rufus."

Whew. That shut her up. I went home to bed. After all, I had agreed to write a good column in the morning, and I needed to honor that agreement.

Jan. 21, 1999

Rufus Opts for Anger

SHE FOUND ME as I waited for the Fourth of July parade to start. I had left my lawn chair to listen to four members of the Sweet Adelines singing group perform on the porch of the Auburn Promenade. When I returned, I found a note on the seat. My husband said he knew nothing about it, just that someone had dropped it and kept going.

"Rushton," I read Rufus T. Firefly's wild scrawl. "Meet me here after the fireworks."

I knew if I didn't, she'd pester me until I did. So that evening we brought two cars downtown for the fireworks, and Don went home afterward. I returned to the stairs in front of the Promenade. In the dark, she almost tripped over me.

"The blood will run when the panther strikes," I said, leaning against the metal railing.

"Funny," she growled, lowering her bulk next to me. "Take the easy way, girl. Laugh. Sure, let's see how you laugh when everything you hold dear is trashed, when the barbarians are at the gates. Then let's see how much you laugh, Rushton! The price of freedom is eternal viligance!"

"Tsk. Get it right, Rufus. You mean vigilance." Then, to stop her sputtering protests, I demanded, "Enough with the political rigmarole. What do you want this time?"

"What do I—Rushton, I want you to take the threat to your well-being seriously! I want you to protest against tyranny, against creeping—"

I made to stand up. "If you can't be specific," I said, "I guess I'll be going."

That got her. She growled. "You're getting wimpy. Didn't you recently write that a way to save the world is to promote lightness? 'There's a place for lightness, silliness,' you wrote. 'Pleasure, too, can save the world, in addition to grave sobriety'? Sweetness and light? Where's your fury, Rushton? Where's your indignation, your outrage, your —"

"Sounds like you're plenty indignant for both of us," I said. "What's got you worked up this time?"

Even in the darkness I could see her face get red. She held out a hand and counted off the items, using some fingers twice. "Look at 'em in Africa, closing their eyes to the AIDS crisis," she growled. "Look at the dopes in the Middle East, warranting the same head-lines week after week for years. Peace talks? Oh, give me a break! Peace, my mother's corset cover!

"And look at the state of health care! Look at the idiotic presidential race! Look at the price of oil! Look at—"

"Oh, come on, Rufus." I rolled my eyes. "You know me better than that. It's easy to get mad if you only pay attention to the stupid stuff. Sure, if you stand and open your arms and invite absurdity by looking for it, you'll have more than enough to get mad at. If you want to get mad and stay mad. But what if you don't? What if—"

"Oh, that's just like you, Rushton, to ignore the obvious. How can you ignore the state of civilization, the idiocy around you? Pushy cell phone users! Conspicuous consumption! Planned obsolescence! Politics as usual! "

"You're like every angry person I know," I said. "You're blind to anything positive, you won't take it seriously and you're ultra-sensitive about the negative, so that's all you focus on. The more you look the more you see, and the madder you get—so all you do is fume. That doesn't help anything.

"Tell me this: What do you do to counteract all this corruption and ugliness?"

Silence. I had another question: "Do you vote?"

"What good does voting do when—"

"Thought so," I said. "Do you recycle? Give blood? Promote birth control? Teach reading?"

"Recycle? Blood? Birth control? Reading? That's your answer?" she shrieked, waving her arms.

"It's one answer," I said. "It's a beginning. At least you'd be contributing. All you do is get angry. I know this is a cliché, but if you don't contribute to the solution, you're part of the problem. Gandhi said it's unlikely nothing you can do will make any difference, but it's very important that you do it. Sure, you can only teach one person to read at a time, give one pint of blood at a time. But you're *doing* something."

"I don't know why I talk to you," she growled, and stalked off. Goody. I went home.

July 13, 2000

Rufus Defines Patriotism

EVERY NIGHT FOR the last couple of months, I've expected to hear from her. After every speech, after every article on anthrax, I eyed the silent phone. After the antiterrorism bill passed, I knew that any minute Rufus T. Firefly would command me to haul myself down to the Clock Tower so she could gloat at me.

And finally... the phone rang. "Hello?" I croaked, sleep still in my voice.

"Sleeping?" Rufus screeched. "How can you sleep at a time like this, when the freedom of the free world is at stake? America's in trouble, Rushton, and you sleep! The price of freedom is eternal vigilance!"

"I can't do anyone any good if I'm tired. Besides," I yawned, "you mean vigilance."

That set her off. She hollered so loud I couldn't keep the phone to my ear. The only way I could shut her up was to agree, once again, to meet her at the Clock Tower.

I found her parked in front of the Tahoe Club, sprawled on the tailgate of a new SUV, arranging boxes in the back. She raised her head as I approached. "That you, Rushton?"

"The blood will run when the panther strikes," I said.

"I swear, Rushton," she growled, "you're going to regret treating this situation so lightly!"

I ignored her. "What is all this?" I asked, inspecting the boxes. "You got a new car, huh? And is that a new big-screen TV? And I see a high-end printer, an oven, a 35mm camera and seven cell phones. What do you need seven cell phones for?"

"My president told me to go shopping, Rushton. So I did."

"Where'd you get the money?"

"I got a second mortgage. It's our patriotic duty to keep the country healthy. I note you're driving the same dusty pickup. Don't you love your country?"

"Is that what you dragged me out here for?"

She scrambled off the tailgate. "I asked you a question, Rushton. Don't you love your country?"

"Yes, Rufus, I love my country," I said. "But going into debt isn't a great way to prove it."

"I don't see you proving it any way," she hissed, glowering at my tired old sandals, my 10-year-old purse. "If you're not on our side, you're on their side."

"You're too intelligent to mouth platitudes at me, Rufus," I lied. "You're saying there's no room for dissension in the ranks? No room for individual thought?"

"How dare you—how can you possibly disagree with the side of freedom?" she demanded. "I can't think of a better way to make the terrorists happy."

"You want to make the terrorists happy?" I sat on her tailgate. "Force people to look upon dissent as treasonous. Even better, push an antiterrorism law through Congress that tosses the concept of a fair trial out the window."

Her face got red. "Damn it, Rushton, that's just meant for non-citizens suspected of acts of terrorism!"

"But the law defines terrorism too broadly," I said. "If your actions adversely affect the citizens or the economy of this country, you can be tried as a terrorist."

"These are terrorists, Rushton! A fair trial's too good for them! We're at war! These are special circumstances!"

"Special circumstances," I agreed. "Except that I fear that once we get used to these special circumstances, they'll reword the law so that it applies to everyone, not just noncitizens. So if Oprah Winfrey badmouths hamburger on TV again, she could be tried as a terrorist. Or if I pay off my credit cards every month. Both might have a negative effect on the economy."

I stood. "Besides, if you think it's OK to try people without having to produce evidence, it's got to be OK with you if somebody puts you on trial in the same situation.

"We should go," I said. "The president says we should be on the lookout for suspicious behavior. Here we are meeting clandestinely in the middle of the night. What if someone reports us for behaving suspiciously?"

She gasped, her eyes shifting from one shadow to another along the street. "It's perfectly innocent," she hissed.

"Then what are you worried about?" I asked, and left her.

Nov. 29, 2001

Rufus and Banned Books

R UFUS HADN'T CALLED me in nearly a year, and I'd been lulled into complacency by her absence. But then I wrote about Banned Books Week. I should have known.

The phone rang as I folded myself into bed. "Rushton!" her raspy voice assaulted my ear. "Don't you know the importance of a united front? Don't you realize that the price of freedom is eternal—uh—watchfulness?"

"You mean vigilance, Rufus," I sighed. "I don't have time to talk to you now."

Her voice rose to a scream, and she didn't calm down until I agreed to meet her downtown.

As I approached East Placer Street, I heard paper tearing. And then I saw her ripping up books. Piles of pages littered the ground around her.

She heard my footsteps and her hands stopped. "That you, Rushton?"

"The blood will run when the panther strikes," I said, and ducked as a pile of pages flew past me.

"I swear, Rushton, someday you'll be sorry you didn't take this battle more seriously," she growled, returning to ripping apart pages. I turned and picked up the shreds and inspected them: pages from the third Harry Potter book.

"What battle is that?" I asked, although I already knew. "And how come you're ripping up Harry Potter?"

"The battle for clean minds," she hissed, reaching for *The Catcher in the Rye*. "Clean minds, moral, virtuous literature, family-friendly libraries, responsible publishers—"

"Your reasoning is unreasonable. It sounds like you just want to censor ideas you disagree with, and destroy books you don't like."

"It's a protest against that evil week that promotes Satanism and pornography," she said.

"Satanism and p—" I dropped the Salinger book and stared at her. "What're you talking about?"

"Banned Books Week, you flaming liberal! That depraved celebration of questionable reading material. This ridiculous observation of banned books is dangerous to the country! It's un-American! It's unpatriotic!"

I sat next to the stack of books on the bench between us and inspected them: *Adventures of Huckleberry Finn, To Kill a Mockingbird, The Great Gilly Hopkins, A Wrinkle in Time, In the Night Kitchen*—even *Where's Waldo?* I'd read them all, and seen them all on the list of banned books at ala.org/advocacy/banned. "Rufus, here's what's dangerous," I said. "Trying to suppress ideas is dangerous. Subverting freedom of speech is dangerous. Insisting you have the right to decide what others can read—that's what's dangerous. That's what's un-American and unpatriotic."

"You don't know what you're talking about!"

"Do you? Have you read any of these?"

"Of course not! Why would I want to pollute my mind with this filth?"

"How do you know they're filthy if you haven't read them? If you haven't read them, how can you presume to pass judgment on them?"

Her hands clenched on Salinger's pages. "People I respect," she started, but I interrupted her.

"People you respect have told you these are terrible books. They have the right to their opinion," I said. "The First Amendment guarantees it. They don't have to read those books if they don't want to. They have the right to keep them from their children. But they don't have the right to keep them from me. And they don't have the right to choose my books for me, or books for other people's children, or what bookstores and libraries can and cannot have on their shelves.

"Besides. I can't think of a better way to interest people in a particular book than by telling them they absolutely must not read it." I got up. "I'm going home. But I have some wonderful parting words for you, from President Eisenhower. 'Don't join the book burners,' he said. 'Don't think you are going to conceal thoughts by concealing evidence that they ever existed.'"

As I walked back to my truck, I had hope. For a whole block, I didn't hear any paper ripping.

###

Sept. 20, 2002

FYI: Banned Books Week is celebrated the last week in September every year.

Big Brother's Eyesight Improves

WHEN SHE PHONED, I didn't recognize her voice at first. Usually Rufus T. Firefly is so adamant and outraged that I know who it is right away. Nobody else calling at 3 A.M. is ever as angry.

But this time my ordinarily crazy lady was calm and easygoing. This time, she kept her voice to tolerable levels. So of course I had trouble realizing who it was. But even odder, she called in the middle of the day.

"What is it, Rufus? I'm busy."

Her chuckle sounded strange in my ear. Rufus chuckling? Rufus tranquil? This was not good news.

"Listen, Rushton, I just want you to know that I'm on your side in this. It's OK with me if you want to attract attention by wandering off alone, demanding time by yourself. I mean, you're an odd duck, but you're harmless. For the most part. That's why I haven't reported you."

"Why would you report me?"

"For being an odd duck, of course. For insisting on your solitude. You don't want people to think you're unpatriotic. You do remember we've all been told to keep our eye out for suspicious behavior?"

"Yeah, but—"

"And you're aware that whenever you hear stories about people who blow up buildings, or take an AK-47 and spray their coworkers, or drown their children one by one, you're also told that they're the misfits, the loners, the ones who stay by themselves?"

"Oh, I see where you're going with this, Rufus. You're telling me I'm a weirdo because I want to be left alone. Thanks a lot."

"You said it, Rushton, I didn't. It's the loners who are the most dangerous, the most untrustworthy, who most often threaten the safety of others. That's what people think when you insist on solitude. There's strength in numbers. We're all in this war on terrorism together, and we all need to fight it together. And the more we stick together, the more we know who's doing what, the better for everybody."

"If you're not with us you're against us?"

"Well, sure. The wisdom of the crowd, Rushton. Like—well, you're aware of the popularity of those reality shows, people put into crazy situations with a camera on them all the time."

"I don't watch reality shows."

Her gasp was satisfying, but I figured she already knew. We go back a ways.

"I hate the idea, Rufus," I said. "For one thing, I think that a purpose of these shows is to convince us that cameras on ordinary people is a good thing. It gets us accustomed to surveillance as benign. It isn't benign."

"That's the liberal in you, Rushton. For decades there was unreasonable reluctance about both hidden and visible cameras. People like you whined about loss of privacy and wanted to be left alone. But now you suspicious oddballs are in the minority, and getting less vocal every day. Better watch out, Rushton. You may not want to be watched, but most others just don't care. And making a fuss about it just attracts attention. Makes people wonder what you have to hide. What are you afraid of?"

"So you're saying that our current pace toward all surveillance, all the time, is a good thing?" I asked. "Good for the country? And that a demand for privacy and solitude signifies potential treachery?"

"Of course."

"I hope you're calling from a cell phone, then."

"Why?" Her tone changed instantly from complacency to wariness.

"Because the feds want global positioning chips in cell phones. If you call 9-1-1, they want wireless carriers to be able to locate you automatically. So Big Brother can already keep track of you, Rufus. As long as you have your phone, the authorities will always have a lock on where you are. You must be greatly reassured. I'll bet you're thrilled, actually."

Clearly, from the sputtering on the other end, she wasn't. Then I heard a loud scraping noise… as if she'd thrown the phone into a garbage can. Excellent. Now I could get back to work.

Feb. 5, 2004

Rufus and Free Speech

RUFUS T. FIREFLY is tiresome at the best of times. But when she's smug, she's insufferable. And she was certainly smug recently when she phoned and woke me up, her voice purring with satisfaction.

"It's a step in the right direction, Rushton, you can't deny it. Congress has listened to the people and they've set things right."

"Rufus, what the—" I couldn't help it, I'd just gotten to sleep and I was exhausted. "What the !@#$%&* are you talking about?"

She snickered. "Better watch your language, Rushton."

"Why? It clearly hasn't hurt you any. You haven't hung up on me, more's the pity."

"Congress doesn't approve of nasty language like that."

I groaned. "Oh, great, Rufus. You're talking about the Broadcast Decency Enforcement Act, aren't you?"

I knew she was smiling. "Which one? But of course it doesn't matter, does it? They both pound nails in the coffins of on-air obscenity and indecency."

In a way, she was right. The Senate's bill, S. 2056, increases the maximum fine for broadcasting "obscene, indecent or profane language" to $275,000. The House bill, H.R. 3717, increases the fine to $500,000.

But I was so-o-o tired. "Rufus, can't we talk about this some other time?" I stretched, trying hard not to disturb Don.

She chuckled. "You can't tell me you're not pleased that you won't be forced to sit through dirty words and indecent subjects when you listen to the radio or watch TV, Rushton. You can't tell me you—"

"Come on, Rufus. Nobody's ever forced me to do that. I've always had the power to change the channel or hit the off button. So have you, comes to that. It's simple. In my opinion, it's a waste of our legislators' time and our tax money for them even to discuss this. I'm embarrassed for them."

"It's a good thing for the country that the rest of the right-thinking American people don't think so. I can hardly wait, Rushton. When these bills become law, we won't have to worry about our children or about our own sensibilities, we won't have to worry about being offended every time we turn on the television."

"But they'll still report on politics and Iraq," I said, yawning. "Talk about offensive. But let me ask you this, Rufus. Who's going to decide what's indecent?"

"What?"

"The bills don't spell that out. Nor do they spell out what qualifies as indecent."

"So what?" she shrieked. "These broadcasters are going to pay for offending me!"

"Think about it," I said. "Since these bills include what they call 'profane language,' what if someone talks extensively about *The Da Vinci Code,* which some feel denigrates the Catholic Church? What if a bunch of viewers finds this discussion profane? Or what if another group finds a news program about abusive priests profane?"

"Don't be ridiculous, Rushton."

"Look up profane in the morning. Check out what it means. But why should the government stop there, Rufus? What's to stop them from silencing anyone who uses language they don't approve of, or discusses subjects they don't want discussed?"

I heard sputtering on the other end of the line. "That would never happen."

"Why not?" I asked. "With no definition of what qualifies as obscene, indecent or profane, and nobody assigned to decide what's obscene and what isn't, the government has as broad a latitude as it has with the Patriot Act, where they can investigate anyone they want and search without a warrant. Not to mention the latitude they've given themselves at Guantánamo Bay, where suspects are imprisoned indefinitely and denied legal advice.

"Rufus," I continued, "if you insist you're such a patriot, why do you so enthusiastically approve of our government trashing our Constitutional rights?"

The crash of a slammed receiver resounded in my ear. Cool! If I could argue Rufus into giving up, I guess I wasn't as tired as I thought.

July 2, 2004

Rufus: Patriotism and Religion

"**W**HAT'S HAPPENED TO Rufus T. Firefly?" Don asked, even though he knew better. "How come she hasn't been around lately?" I shuddered, and wasn't surprised last Sunday when the phone rang in the middle of the night. I rolled over and picked up the receiver.

"What, Rufus?" I muttered.

"I see the president feels sorry for you," she shouted. I winced, and jerked the receiver from my ear.

"Hmmm?" I yawned. "What do you want, Rufus? I'm tired. I work for a living, remember?"

"There you go," she hissed, "denigrating our president and his faith again. That's just like you."

"I give you ten seconds—no, five, Rufus. Then I'm hanging up. What do you want?"

"You're going to force me to compress 2,000 years of sincere belief into five seconds? Rushton, you don't deserve—"

I couldn't help it. I hung up on her. But I knew what would happen, so started to dress. I would have to meet her downtown, or it would be a long night of hanging up on her. I had just tied my shoes when the phone rang again.

When I reached the Clock Tower, I found her quietly waiting. No boxes surrounded her, no piles of newspaper. Only one news story lay on the bench beside her.

She heard me approach. "Rushton?"

"The blood will run when the panther strikes," I said, tired of this conversation already, whatever its focus.

"You poor sap, Rushton," she snarled. "If the president hadn't offered his excuses for people like you—"

"I'm sorry, I don't get it, Rufus—"

"Oh, you know, at his press conference in April," she said, waving impatiently. "Where he said even if you don't worship, you're still an American."

"Oh, for heaven's sake, is that what this is about? And you think this has something to do with me?"

"Of course it does, Rushton. He acknowledged with great compassion that people like you are just as American as if you were a good Christian, someone who worships God."

"Well," I said evenly, perching on the bench, "how sad that he felt the need to say that at all. What was it? Do you have it there?"

She picked up the story beside her and read from it, smugness in her voice: "'The great thing about America is that you should be allowed to worship any way you want. And if you choose not to worship, you're equally as patriotic as somebody who does worship. And if you choose to worship, you're equally American if you're a Christian, a Jew, a Muslim.'"

I took a deep breath. "Any way I want? If I can worship any way I want, that means I have carte blanche to sacrifice virgins, Rufus. Is that OK with you? What if a church's worship rituals involve burning books that disagree with its doctrine? Both those have to be OK with you—and the president, since he says we should be allowed to worship any way we want."

She was shaking with rage. But she held her temper, and only said, "You're lucky you live here, Rushton, where you're free to believe, or not believe—"

"You mean if I choose not to worship, I'm just as patriotic as someone who does? How odd and unfortunate that patriotism and religion should have gotten so mixed up together. They're separate entities."

"Of course you'd say that, Rushton, you infidel—"

"Me, an infidel? You know the definition of an infidel? Somebody without faith. An irreligious person. But I'm not irreligious. I have a religion. It's just not your religion."

"But—you don't worship—"

"How do you know, Rufus? You have no idea whether I worship, or what, or who or how or why or how often. You don't know, because I believe religion is a private matter. It's none of anybody's business. I'm not the only one who thinks so, either. I don't have a Bible with me, but in several places both Christ and God say that one should keep one's religion to oneself.

"And it's a shame," I said as I stood and hunted for my truck key, "that more people don't pay attention to that admonishment. The world would be a good deal calmer."

That kept her quiet long enough for me to reach the truck and drive away. Thank God.

###

May 5, 2005

A Matter of National Security

RUFUS T. FIREFLY hadn't contacted me in years, it seemed. But every time George Bush signed an executive order, I shivered, anticipating a gloating phone call. The afternoon I chatted politely with a member of Veterans for Peace, I expected to hear from Rufus, scolding me for being courteous to a liberal. The night Don and I came home after watching a politically-tinged movie in Nevada City, I was sure she'd call.

But no. Either she'd given up on me, or she was just biding her time.

Turns out she was just biding her time. Just as I was falling asleep the other night, the phone rang. I answered it. It could have been a relative. But it wasn't, and I knew it immediately.

"Rushton?" came the dreaded, raspy voice.

"Oh, lord," I muttered. "Rufus? What do you want?"

"Do you know how much trouble you're in?" she demanded. "You have too many suspicious conversations. Your behavior is suspect. If you don't want me to alert the authorities, tell me why I shouldn't."

"Maybe you should just alert the authorities," I said.

"Don't you get it? What's the matter with you? You seem to think it's perfectly OK to talk to whoever you want to about anything, from politics and President Bush to the Iraq war and the economy. We can't afford to let traitors get the upper hand!"

I knew she wouldn't shut up until I agreed to meet her at the Clock Tower. It briefly occurred to me to just say I'd be there and go back to sleep instead, but I knew she'd never let me get away with it. So 20 minutes later, I approached her where she sat on her usual bench.

She heard me. "Rushton?"

"Blood will run when the panther strikes," I said, yawning.

She winced. "This isn't funny," she hissed. "The price of liberty is eternal viligance."

"Geez, Rufus, get it right. The word is vigilance."

As she controlled herself with an effort, she dug into a pocket and pulled out a sheaf of papers. "If you don't want to be thought of as an evil-doer sympathizer," she said, "you'd better have good reasons for this behavior."

I sat next to her. "Let me see, please," I said, attempting to read what she had on her lap. But she snatched it away.

"You don't have the right to see this if you're suspected of being a sympathizer," she said.

"Is that how it is? OK, what am I accused of?"

"None of your business," she said.

"I see where this is going," I said. "If we were in a courtroom, this would be unconstitutional. But if you had your way, I'd be down in Guantánamo, without access to an attorney, no knowledge of what I'm accused of, and no chance to confront my accusers. Talk about unpatriotic."

"Don't talk to me about patriotism, Rushton. You talked with your doctor, numerous friends, relatives and coworkers about how much you don't like Bush! Any time the president's name comes up, you take the side of the evil-doers."

"So if I'm not with you, I'm against you? You're making it a black and white issue, and it isn't, Rufus. Dissent is an American value, whether you like it or not. I can—and do—love America while taking issue with how my president is undermining the Constitution."

"Rushton!" She slapped her thigh with the papers. "What's more important—spreading democracy and insuring people's freedom, or your questionable right to question your president?"

"I don't think it's questionable, Rufus. Plus, I think it's nuts to try to insure people's freedom by curtailing it." I stood and stretched. "Anyway, pretty soon I think you'll be seeing things my way."

"What do you mean?"

"You know how people in power like to hold onto that power. When the pendulum swings back and the Democrats regain the White House, do you think they'll be willing to restore the rights the Republicans took away? I don't think so. So when you're outraged at what the Democrats are doing, you'll have to watch your mouth—or risk becoming a target of warrantless surveillance. But that must be all right with you, since it's all right with you when the Republicans exert that power."

That shut her up good. It was thrilling. At home, I fell asleep with a pleasant memory of her shocked face.

Aug. 19, 2007

four

Technology

HURRAY FOR TECHNOLOGY! *Yes, yes, yes, I agree. My computer's wonderful. I love my answering machine. Also other people's. Plus, I'm old enough to remember a time when if you wanted another copy of something, you used carbon paper or typed the thing again. And if you changed your mind once you'd finished, you typed the thing again. Or if you recognized you'd made a mistake, you typed the thing again. No, I wouldn't go back to a typewriter, thank you very much.*

But because I'm not unique, I know I'm not the only one to worry that, even as technology makes life easier (most of the time, for most of us), it insidiously encourages separation, making it harder to be with one another.

Of course, I suppose this is a good thing. After all, it just means face-to-face interaction and communication and friendships are more important than ever.

If Print Dies, Who Will Miss It?

"**P**ROGRESS HAS NEVER been a bargain," intones Spencer Tracy in Stanley Kramer's wonderful *Inherit the Wind,* from 1960. "You've got to pay for it. Sometimes I think there's a man behind a counter who says, 'Yes, you may have a telephone, but you'll have to give up privacy, and the charm of distance. Madam, you may vote, but at a price: you lose the right to retreat behind a powder-puff or a petticoat. Mister, you may conquer the air. But the birds will lose their wonder, and the clouds will smell of gasoline.'"

Of course, only those who observe this progress are aware of paying for it. Only the person who consciously gave up the charm of distance is aware of the sacrifice he made by installing a telephone. Those umpteen generations who come after him are only conscious of how terrific it is to have a phone—if they think about the phone at all.

And print? What about letters on a page? A page, as in a piece of paper? Well... we've been hearing obituaries for print for years. Print—as in newspapers, newsletters, magazines and books. Print is dead. Long live the silicon chip.

Maybe it's true. I hate to think this way, but maybe the print media are all poised to crash, eventually to be replaced by hand-held Walkman- and Gameboy-like computers that you can program to scan a daily network of news, trivia, sports and information all originating from one databank centralized in Chicago.

Why not? Remember when the pocket calculators first came out? They cost $500 for a machine the size of a thick paperback, capable of adding, subtracting, multiplying and dividing and not much else. And now? Companies practically give them away at $25 a pop, these thin, multi-buttoned would-be abacuses that perform any calculation you might take it into your head to figure—and plenty that you won't.

So maybe that will happen with print. It'll all get transferred onto a hand-held screen, any word you want accessible by button, and nobody will have any use for page after cumbersome page of 14 by 22 newsprint that clutters up both the environment and your breakfast table. Why should libraries squander all that real estate when you could access any information you might want by pressing a button on a screen in your hand? Surely all those soon-to-be-obsolete bookstores and newsstands could be put to better use, too. Maybe by selling Readmans, pocket fax machines and Handipedias.

And if that happens, so what? Oh, well. We've had earth-shattering changes before, and the world has continued to turn on its axis. We switch from horses to automobiles. "White only" water fountains vanish. Scientists find a vaccine for polio. Ted Turner colorizes *The Maltese Falcon*.

Yet in spite of these revolutionary changes, our blood continues to circulate, people still fall in love, merchants still hose off their sidewalks and couples still argue about who will take out the garbage.

So, really, what difference will it make if print dies the same slow demise as vaudeville, 1930s radio, *Look* magazine and the metal Log Cabin Syrup cans? After one or two generations, who'll miss it?

In this battle my opinion doesn't count. Partly because I'm so old and set in my ways, but mainly because I stand to lose so much. *Of course she'd say that,* I hear my opponents scoff. *She makes a living from print. How shortsighted of her.*

So whatever I say concerning the possible demise of print is suspect. My motives are selfish. But take me seriously anyway.

I suppose I can get used to holding plastic instead of paper, punching buttons rather than turning pages, pulling out my Readman instead of trekking to the library, bookstore or newsstand.

I can, but I'd rather not. The alternatives to print seem so cold, so isolated and disconnected. The price for progress seems too high.

But that makes no difference. I wish it did, but it never has.

Sept. 9. 1993

FYI: "So maybe that will happen with print. It'll all get transferred onto a hand-held screen… Readmans, pocket fax machines and Handipedias." Hmmm. No, impossible. Never happen.

Who's Watching the Children?

I'VE SAID THIS before: We get used to what we're used to. What's familiar early on becomes comfortable, basic and ordinary.

I'm not alone in this awareness. If you want to change the world, you start with the kids. Disney did it. Microsoft did it. The fast food companies are doing it. Like racism, sexism and religious intolerance, to learn it well, you learn it early. You have to be carefully taught.

Now consider the ubiquitous trappings of instant communication: pagers, answering machines, faxes, cell phones and email. You may not have grown up with all this. But your kids have. They're used to it.

Recently I saw a news story about a children's bracelet fitted with a global positioning system. It can pinpoint the wearer's location within a few feet and triggers an alarm if removed. Parents worried about their children's safety can strap one of these babies on and track their kids via the Internet.

I don't mind telling you this makes me very itchy. I can see beyond that damn little three-ounce bracelet.

First of all, this is taking advantage of parents' paranoia, inflaming it, convincing them that the way to make their children safe is to spend more money rather than spend more time with them.

This is like television—another artificial babysitter.

Second, it's a short hop from this wristwatch-sized tracker to, say, implanting a GPS chip in your child's earlobe. It could be sold as the next child-safety insurance. Imagine the clever marketing, going right for the jugular: "You're the right kind of parent. What good parent wouldn't want the best for her child?"

Getting children accustomed to being under surveillance is just that: getting them accustomed to being under surveillance. Get children used to it and it becomes ordinary, just part of the landscape. Your battle is won. And bam—you've changed the world.

Who would benefit from such a radical change? How about corporate America? If you fret about companies invading your privacy now, consider how much more of a nuisance they'd be if they could track you.

Even worse, think of the FBI, IRS, DEA and the CIA, just a few on a very long list. Imagine how delighted they'd be if they could click a button and follow you. They could question the patriotism of those who wanted to be left alone. *Got something to hide, do you?*

I'd love to accept everything at face value, trust everything I hear. It would be so comforting not to have an imagination, not to let my brain simmer, not to follow all these terrible tendrils of suspicion that lead me to places I'd rather not go.

But you know the old saying: Just because you're paranoid doesn't mean they're not following you.

Aug. 29, 2002

The High Price of Isolation

A S I TURNED onto the frontage road from the freeway, I saw a woman walking in the same direction. She lugged a big bag of groceries in one arm and a toddler in another. She walked slowly and stopped often, shifting that little boy around on her hip. She looked little and alone by the side of the road, with what must have seemed like miles to go.

She needed help. So when I could, I made a U-turn and headed back. I stopped where she could see me and approached her with a smile and offered her a ride. She asked where I was going, and I told her I'd take her wherever she wanted, because she looked like she had her hands full.

She was tempted. Standing there in the afternoon sun with the freeway rush all around us, I saw her consider: a driver and a car right there, her son and that night's dinner and those apples and the gallon of milk growing heavier in her arms and home all those steps away...

But she said no, very pleasantly and politely, but very firmly. Nonplused, I pushed her a little, said something like *really? It's no problem, love to do it—*

Nice, try, Susan. But she didn't know me. I'd just suddenly appeared. Maybe she'd have felt different if she only had groceries in her arms. But she had her son to worry about. And as big a hassle as it was to get the two of them home by walking, at least they were safe. At least she had control of the situation.

Standing there in the afternoon sun with the freeway rush all around us, I saw her not trust me. There was nothing I could do about it.

I felt awful. I felt dishonest and corrupt, even though I was neither. In spite of my innocence, guilt for heinous crimes yet uncommitted—even unconsidered—swam in me. I know she saw that guilt.

Chastened, I walked back to my car. That was my first punishment. My second was seeing her image in my rear-view mirror, struggling again with her son and her groceries.

This was several years ago. Since then, I've mistrusted strangers too, solely because they're strangers. Like that young mother, I consider my safety more important than someone else's feelings. I check who's behind me. I stop and go the other way. I won't open my screen door to take a brochure.

I'm not alone. All around me, everywhere, every day, people mistrust strangers. And most of the time, most of these strangers have done nothing to earn that mistrust—except that they're strangers. Most are as innocent of heinous crimes as I am, but it doesn't matter. People do commit heinous crimes; better to chance someone else's hurt feelings than to chance heinousness.

But I think about that young mother sometimes, consider how awful I felt, and how unreasonably guilty. And that's happened just once to me. Once was enough. Consider the pounding men get, though, every day, how careful they have to be, too, and the accusing looks they get just because they're men.

I know there's a solution to this, but things aren't moving in that direction.

You've seen those AT&T commercials, touting the future: *ever gotten directions without getting out of your car? You will.* You've heard the news stories about modems allowing you to work from home. You know about CD-ROM hardware as well as the Internet, both of which connect you with millions of pages of information that you formerly had to get out of the house and go to the library to read.

While I truly couldn't exist without the microchip, I find myself eyeing all this new stuff warily. As handy as it is, technology isolates people. New technology separates them even more, and gets them used to being separated. People lose the knack of being with and around each other. The result is more distrust and uneasiness—thus more encouragement to be separate.

The result of that? More of those looks like I got from that woman by the side of the road. More misplaced guilt feelings.

Who needs it? If we want to, we can do better than that.

###

Jan. 20, 1994

The Result of Technology

I TEM: *AT LEAST three companies have designed video software that recognizes and eliminates any reference to immoral, sexual or violent activity.* Here at Defdummenblynde Technologies, we know what the American family wants. Today's American family wants wholesome family entertainment, harmless, family-oriented movies and television and family-friendly, inoffensive Internet access.

American parents don't want to have to explain anything to their children. American parents want to be sure that they can leave their children in front of the TV and know that their children won't see anything violent or provocative.

With Defdummenblynde, parents don't need to worry. No longer must you sit with your children to monitor their television watching. No longer will you be subjected to embarrassing questions. So what if *The French Connection* is on tonight? So what if your religious faith precludes hearing the dangerous Satanic messages in the Harry Potter movie?

With the groundbreaking and unique Defdummenblynde C-Noweevel software, you can leave your children alone with any video, secure in the knowledge that regardless of the original content, they will see and hear nothing offensive.

Imagine! No weapons, no bad language, no nudity. With the Noweevel software, instead of the distasteful violence in, say, *The*

Wizard of Oz, your children can watch the movie without ever seeing, or hearing references to, witches of any sort, since witches have no part in a wholesome life.

Even better for your peace of mind, the C-Noweevel software eliminates the two grisly deaths, because what could be more terrifying to an impressionable mind than a house crushing someone? Or a young girl killing someone—even accidentally?

The cutting-edge C-Noweevel software not only eliminates the ugly violence, it removes rude language, including rude tones of voice, so harmful to impressionable minds, so anti-family. Consider, for example, the harsh exchange between Dorothy and the Wizard, where she scolds him for scaring the Lion, and he shouts "Silence, whippersnapper!" Gone, as if it never existed.

Indeed, the C-Noweevel software seeks out and eliminates behavior that might undermine the sanctity of the family. So of course Dorothy never argues with her aunt and uncle. To hear her behaving otherwise would plant anti-family ideas in children's heads.

Yes, Defdummenblynde Technologies offers families what they've always wanted: children's movies and fairy tales without the sex and violence. Imagine, finally, Sleeping Beauty without the fierce prince and the horrifying dragon; Shirley Temple movies without her continually stamping her feet at authority; Snow White without the immorality of one unchaperoned young woman living in sin with seven old men—oh, we can go on and on.

And with the innovative C-Noweevel T2Z upgrade, available soon, you can make sure that your children will see nothing unseemly on television programs.

You don't have to forbid your children from watching the Three

Stooges anymore. The C-Noweevel software turns a 20-minute short into a five-minute sequence of the three men just standing there. Talk about wholesome!

You don't have to be anxious about the kids inadvertently hearing a story on the 6 o'clock news of a sniper gone mad in Chicago, or waking up early from a nap and hearing people screaming at each other on Rikki Lake, or taking advantage of your absence to check out AMC's screening of *The Godfather*.

C-Noweevel makes it simple! Not only simple, it makes things harmless. You don't have to watch or pay attention to your children, ever again. Even better, you can keep your television on all the time!

Jan. 1, 2002

Resistance to Technology

O H, I'M SO old-fashioned. Last week I looked up a Loomis address on the Internet. I found it, called the place and set up a time to go visit. And then—because I needed to have the address in front of me in the car—I found a piece of paper and wrote down the information. I mean I rifled my desk drawer for a pencil. Geez, I could have pressed the printable version right there on the screen. But no, I wrote it down. By hand.

I've written quite a bit lately about how technology is surrounding us. And it's only going to get worse. Or better, depending on your attitude.

After all, everyone younger than I is used to it. My 6-year-old niece, for example, tells me her favorite part of kindergarten is when they go to the computers. I tell her when I was her age, I had to walk 10 miles in the snow to get to my computer lab.

I have a lot of problems with technology, and by that I don't mean that I can't get stuff to work the way I want it to. I can't, but that's not it.

No, I mean I distrust it. A lot of it, anyway, although I'm on the Internet all the time, looking for information. It makes me uneasy. Because anyone can post anything anywhere, and there's no regulation, no checks.

Worse, I hate the invasive ads. If you think they're terrible on television, spend some time on the Internet. Egad, they drive me nuts. And I have the impression that the technological goal is to put TV in the palm of your hand, thus making those ads even more intimate. What sitting ducks your kids will be.

Oh well, it's great for the economy.

Another unnerving aspect of technology is what experts—even non-experts—can do with photography. Yes, I know, retouching's always been around. Fakery and staging are basic elements of the art.

You may have seen a group photo of jazz artists taken in Harlem in 1958. I just found it by searching online for Harlem Jazz. And there they all are, posed on the street in front of an old brownstone. Now here's a wild thought—I'll bet everyone in that picture was there the day they took the photo. Ya think?

Not like today. Today you can drop anyone you want into a photo, alter the lighting, change someone's clothes, delete someone, move 'em around, change the hairstyle, insert a baby in someone's arms, on and on.

Makes me suspicious of "official photos." I have no other hard evidence that these two people ever met, much less looked at each other or shook hands. Yet somebody wants me to believe they've agreed on something. Why?

It's too easy to fool people. And it's getting even easier.

I just saw *Charlotte's Web,* for example. Yeah, that charming kids' fantasy. I sat in the dark and looked at Dakota Fanning holding a pig, and as I looked I wondered if they really filmed her holding a pig. Or did they put the pig in there later? Sure looked like she was holding a pig.

I know. It's only a movie. Just a kids' movie… starring a talking spider and a horse with Robert Redford's voice. You don't have to tell me. I thought the same thing as I recognized my cynicism.

But my unbridled cynicism also makes me wonder about the video that supposedly shows Saddam Hussein's death. No, I haven't seen it. But consider how easily someone could create that image. Geez, it's child's play.

Not that I could do it. But you know, I'll bet Dakota Fanning could.

###

Jan. 7, 2007

Living in the 3D World

UBIQUITOUS TECHNOLOGY SURROUNDS us, rules us, captivates us, and it's not going away. Get with it. Use it. Learn it. Like it or not.

Like it or not? Come on, Rushton. What's not to like?

Oh, gee whiz. Let me count the ways. Do you know I've used the same cell phone since 2006? I can't help it. It still works. I can call someone and leave a message. I can retrieve messages from my machine at home. Why should I replace it?

Yes, it's miserly people like me who keep slowing the economy. If only I'd race out and buy new TVs, new laptops, new cameras, new phones, new Kindles, new iPads. All the stuff I have is obsolete. What's the matter with me? Why do I keep dragging my heels?

It's hard to turn away from my window, gazing as the long day wanes, the slow moon climbs. I suppose I could see the same thing on my computer or my plasma TV—if I'd ever break down and buy one. After all, the new HDTVs make everything look so lifelike.

The thing is, life itself is pretty lifelike. If I pay attention only to what's available via microchips, I miss the real stuff. Just like that guy last week in the post office parking lot who moseyed in front of me, ignoring my approaching pickup as he checked messages on his smartphone. The dope.

Actually, his behavior encouraged me to start paying more attention to the real stuff. Last weekend as the sun blazed through the kitchen window onto my just-poured coffee, I watched the patterns that appeared on the hot surface, dancing, racing, disappearing here and popping up somewhere else. How fascinating. How beautiful. How uncomputerized and undigital.

At the Library on Wednesday, I saw two boys from E.V. Cain, each holding something that looked at first like a skateboard. But no. As I got closer, their contraptions resembled bookends with spiral-shaped gizmos connected to each end.

It was a familiar shape. "Excuse me," I said. "Is that DNA?"

They allowed as how it was.

How cool is that, I thought, thanking them. I didn't learn about DNA until I was a junior in high school. And they're learning about it better than I did, building this model—a physical model, mind you.

Their learning about DNA may have involved an integrated circuit, but creating these models also involved useful but extremely old-fashioned things like nails and paper and glue and wood.

As I drove away, I noticed a couple of young men at the top of the stairs to the Library Garden Theater, playing their acoustic guitars. I saw another arriving to join them. Acoustic guitars, mind you. Not electric.

And parking in the Wells Fargo lot on High Street, I saw the knot of people milling around the bicycle-car accident that you read about Thursday morning.

EMTs hovered over the boy on the ground as a cop directed traffic. Another sprayed paint around the crumpled bike. The fire engine's lights blinked and the engine rumbled. And as I watched, I didn't see anybody checking email, making a phone call or jiggling to the beat of music on his iPod.

This was real life. People were paying attention to it.

I'm going to do more of that, even though there's no app for it. Care to join me?

Feb. 27, 2011

The Personal Touch Still Matters

MODERN? ME? WELL, sure. After all, I have a cell phone. I work on a computer. But I'm also, I confess, old-fashioned. I read newspapers. I even write for a newspaper. Plus I read books. Books. You know, those things you hold in your hands? With all those pages that you turn just by using your fingers?

I'm not alone in my reluctance to embrace everything newfangled and modern. As evidence, I offer you a photograph—both online and in a newspaper—that confuses me and gives me hope. On Oct. 18, in response to the death of Steve Jobs, people covered the windows of the Apple Store in Palo Alto with scraps of paper, all of them expressing condolences on the loss of this visionary.

This didn't happen only in Palo Alto. Photos of the identical baffling phenomenon popped up in New York City, Houston, Boston, Montreal, Japan and Hong Kong. Thousands of Jobs' fans chose to express their sorrow by writing something. On a piece of paper. With a writing implement.

Do you find that amazing? I do. I mean, this is the 21st century. The death of the guy who introduced the Mac, the iPad, the iPhone and the iPod—and thus trained people to abandon paper and pens—resulted in people using paper. And pens. So they could write things down. With their hands, excuse the expression.

Sorry. I just can't get over it. Why didn't people use their iPhones to take photos of their condolence notes on their iPads and stick those up, instead?

I guess they figured that when you want to say something from the heart, a screen with words in 10-point Arial just feels too impersonal. Gee. Impersonal. In 2011? Who'd have thunk it?

Grady Hesters understands. "If I want to say something with significant emotional content," he said, "I don't feel comfortable communicating only electronically." Especially when he's sharing something deeply personal.

"I write thank you notes all the time," said Horti Childs. "I hand-write them. With a fountain pen." A fountain pen, for goodness' sake. "You want to tell people thank you," she said. "And writing it down means something."

Jim Lawson uses a hammer that belonged to his father. "It's at least 60 years old," he said. Wow. Talk about old fashioned. And when he uses it, he not only thinks of his dad, "but I think of his work ethic, too. He was a very hard worker, conscientious and honest."

And Jim's wife Judy Gordon-Lawson, owner of Mountain Mama in Auburn Town Center, visits her mother in Connecticut every couple of months. She could just get Skype, I guess, and visit her that way. In these ultra-modern times. "But I like to spend time with her," she said. "And we play cards. Everyone enjoys the social interaction and the challenge of a good game."

I approached Cindy Ditman at the Auburn Library. In addition to getting books (books!) from the library, she and her daughters "like to do a lot of baking," she said when I asked if she does anything she considers old-fashioned. "And we do crafts and work in the garden. And we try to make gifts when we can."

Also at the library, I met David Stryker. He sat next to a stack of audiobooks—a relatively newfangled concept. He acknowledged that even more newfangled is the possibility of downloading them and listening to them in his car, but he doesn't have the equipment necessary. "My life doesn't revolve around the latest and greatest available from Apple," he said.

At Depoe Bay, barista and writer Matt Reeves said, "I hate staring at a screen. I use a pen and paper when I write. It just flows out more that way."

So—what's Steve Jobs doing? Spinning in his grave? After all, he and Apple spent billions on advertising, billions in research and development, and years exhorting people to Think Different (sic). But when people need to express themselves with sincerity, they abandon the silicon chip and go for paper and pen. Astonishing.

And encouraging.

Oct. 30, 2011

Retreating from the Future

OR ALL INTENTS and purposes and from all accounts, you'd
think I live in the 21st century. Just like you do. I check my
email. I have an answering machine. I have a cell phone. I use a
credit card. I listen to audiobooks. My truck has airbags and fuel in-
jection. See? What's so 1970s about that?

But let me tell you what I did last Wednesday. You remember
that windy, rainy day, snow in the mountains and in Foresthill. I'd
written some letters—yes... written. Some letters. You remember
those. But at least I didn't use a typewriter. Give me that. Plus, I
knew exactly which buttons to press to print them out.

Anyway, I wanted to be sure these letters got to people. So I delivered them. Personally. I walked into where these people worked.
And I handed them over. It felt personal and right and friendly and
intimate. I looked at the people I gave them to. They looked at me. I
smiled, they smiled. I spoke, they spoke.

Yes, I know. I stood face to face with these people. How old-
fashioned. How can I call myself a modern woman?

Well, I guess I can't. You know I can't—I've muttered and ha-
rangued for years about iPods and iPads and laptops and texting
and iPhones and Kindles and fancy ringtones. Years ago I heard
about a guy who wanted to know the instant he received an email,
no matter where he was or what he was doing. So he had a chip

embedded in his skin. I guess the chip vibrates or something—burns, tickles, hums "Oh, Susannah"—when he gets an email.

Boy. He must really be important. Or at least he thinks he's important. So important that he has to be at somebody's beck and call 24/7. The poor guy. How dreary.

But here's the thing. I anticipate all of us will have to emulate him. Somehow. Sooner or later.

Last January, I saw reports in the media about the International Consumer Electronics Show in Las Vegas. A plethora of groundbreaking products debuted at this high-tech event, with all the expected la-di-dah hoopla and skimpily dressed models. Among them: contact lenses that allow you to read your emails and view the Internet even as you're crossing the street, eating dinner, watching a movie, driving. Making love.

Hot dog.

They call it augmented reality information. Not reality. Reality information.

Since then, I've seen eyeglasses that offer the same fancy concept.

So I have seen the future, and it's unnerving.

I mean, think about it. It's hard to find music CDs anymore—you have to download music. I predict the same with DVDs. If you want to apply for a job, you have to go online. Post offices are closing. So, to my immense dismay, are bookstores. Phone booths have gone the way of Nehi.

Scoff if you must, but I anticipate a time when those contact lenses will be the only way to read email. If you find this exciting, please stay away from me. Good grief—it's surreal enough now, dodging all these people conversing through the ether as they bump into all these people staring at their iPhones and texting.

You think I'm overstating the case? Well, the last time I went to an aquarium, I saw a mother gasp with delight at a vibrant fish and urge her daughter to look at its colors.

"Take a picture, Mom," murmured the girl, sighing hugely. She'd look at the augmented reality information later. When she had no texting to do.

See why I'm unnerved? See why I delivered my letters in person? I want to keep that future—with its augmented reality—where it belongs. In the future. If that's the 21st century, you can have it. Thanks anyway. I'd rather look at people and smile.

March 4, 2012

five

First Amendment

I LOVE THE First Amendment. I love the Bill of Rights in general, but I especially have a soft spot for the First Amendment. It covers an immense territory in only 45 words: "Congress shall make no law respecting an establishment of religion, or prohibiting the free exercise thereof; or abridging the freedom of speech, or of the press; or the right of the people peaceably to assemble, and to petition the Government for a redress of grievances."

Selfish? Of course I'm selfish. The First Amendment makes life easier for me. I don't have to worship a god I don't believe in (neither do you), I can write and say what I please without looking over my shoulder (so can you) and I can read what I please. So can you. For the moment.

If the subject touches on one of these—religion or speech or writing, the media or aiming a magnifying glass at my leaders—the column is very likely here.

Don't Read This—It's Offensive

O N MY 10th birthday, my best friend gave me a copy of *Little Women*. My mother was thrilled. She extolled its wonderfulness and insisted I'd love it. As I listened, my heart sank. Clearly, reading it would be good for me.

Oh, sure. I wouldn't let her trap me into wholesomeness that easily. I wouldn't touch it, even when I found *Auntie Mame* on the shelf and she said I couldn't read it until I finished Louisa May Alcott. Finally, after I'd devoured *Auntie Mame* at least twice, my mother admitted that her approval would only ensure that I'd leave the thing alone.

Then she sailed off in the opposite direction. When I was 13, she bought and read *Candy,* a book I'd never heard of, by Terry Southern, an author who meant nothing to me. She burned it in disgust. How do I know? She told me.

At once, I hunted up this book she thought so terrible. Its awfulness was beyond my comprehension, as were most of the words I scurried to the dictionary to decipher. I'll let you imagine them. But even their definitions left me mystified.

But so what? She didn't want me to read it, so I did. I'd never have considered it if she hadn't told me not to. In her defense, I was her first child. She'd never had a 13-year-old before.

So the two of us learned what people keep discovering, generation after generation, in spite of all the well-documented evidence over the previous centuries: Tell someone not to read something and in 20 minutes the piece is guaranteed to be dog-eared and underlined.

Even more predictable is that the fuss you make promotes the cause you're fighting against. Ban a book in Boston? Bookstores elsewhere sell out instantly. Forbid a high school class from reading *Catcher in the Rye* or *Huckleberry Finn* and suddenly there's a waiting list in the library.

When Henry Miller wrote *Topic of Cancer* and *Tropic of Capricorn,* the commotion made over them, from the Postmaster General on down, created reams of publicity and a brisk black market. Henry Miller became a household word. Is that what the protesters had in mind?

It's not just books, either. In 1980 the Moral Majority attempted to shut down a Maryland bakery it accused of selling anatomically correct gingerbread men to minors. Oh, such a fuss. During the furor in the courts and the media, the owner of the shop said that she expected to triple her sales as a result of the free publicity.

This has happened endless times in the past, and it will continue to happen. It drives me crazy. I shake my head when I hear people protesting a movie, shrieking about a comedian or censoring rock lyrics. The inevitable result? It's like minting money. Producers and rock stars rake in the dough.

Yet I know these protesters have a right and a responsibility to speak out.

I have that same responsibility, but I'm not sure how to exercise it. I hate movies that laugh at violence toward women, as much as I mutter and chafe at comedians who ridicule ethnic groups.

It's a complex problem. It rankles to remain silent, implying approval, yet I know what can happen if I start yelling.

Wait—I know. How about if I endorse the thing I hate? Yes, that's it! Give those comedians my wholehearted, unconditional approval. Insist that their message is healthful and virtuous, *good* for America. If this middle-aged, conservatively dressed, middle-class woman with no tattoos shouts it loudly enough, I'll stop their careers dead in the water.

Or I could hire a conservative public figure or organization to sanction them, somebody or some group noted for an extravagant devotion to the wholesome. What would happen if the PTA came out earnestly and enthusiastically endorsing a movie containing gratuitous sexual scenes? Would anyone under 25 see that film?

To repeat: If you make a public fuss, you help the cause you're fighting against. Telling people that they shouldn't look at, hear, belong to, or read something because it's offensive just doesn't work.

Want proof? How well did it work with you, you who were warned that you mustn't read this?

May 1988

FYI: I still haven't read Little Women. *I've seen each of the several movies made from the book, but that's it.*

I Swear!

S WEARING'S LIKE VOODOO—it works because we believe it and we believe it because it works. We've agreed that certain words have the power to offend. Because we agree they're offensive, they are.

Consider the swear words you know. They fall into three basic categories: references to religion, parental heritage and the body.

I can imagine the beginnings of religious curses, back in the foggy mists of time. People knew less and feared more. So much happened that made so little sense, that nobody could explain—tornadoes, earthquakes, volcanoes, tooth decay—it seemed obvious that the gods acted either on whimsy or at the behest of anyone who called upon them.

To swear by Jove or Jehovah must have made the speaker's motive seem more respectable. And when one got angry, it added to the force of that anger to bring another, greater, power along. Maybe nothing would happen if you called on that god in your anger. But maybe it would. If your enemy lost his arm after his confrontation with you, then, surely, your enemies would take you and your anger more seriously.

On the other hand, I've always found it curious that casting aspersions on one's mother has been an effective, agreed-upon method to disparage someone. Why his mother, I wonder? Why not his father? Maybe the speaker felt that if word got back about those insults, there was little chance of getting beat up by the guy's mother.

But sometimes it's difficult to pinpoint who one's father is. Usually only two people are present at a conception, and both of them can lie later. However, since there are usually more witnesses at a birth, people are always pretty sure whose womb you slid out of. It's easier to insult someone if you know her name, so—simple, badmouth your mother.

It's hard enough to tolerate slurs against your mother. But wouldn't you find it insulting if someone disparaged your father? But nobody ever sneers "Yo' papa" at you. I don't understand why "son of a bachelor" never caught on.

As strange as mother insults are, even odder and quirkier are the swear words referring to the body. Consider them: They deal with either the bathroom or the bedroom.

I can understand about bathroom references. After all, our bodies find those excretions poisonous and we must dispose of them. So of course we would find allusions to them useful when we need to insult someone.

But those bedroom references? I don't get it. Over the eons sex kept us around, kept us a species; why would references to it be insulting? Plus—and I imagine I'm not alone in this—the process feels so good.

But no. Those parts and actions necessary for reproduction— they're the nouns and verbs of choice when we want real fighting words, insults to push even the most easygoing into throes of rage.

Yet—they're very near and dear to us. We cherish the existence of the birds and the bees, don't we? Even so, we use words referring to this process when we seek to reduce an opponent to shreds.

They're all so terrible as to make one shudder deliciously with the badness of it—only because everybody agrees that they're all so terrible. I'm right, admit it. How far will you get in that barroom brawl calling someone a shoulder blade?

What's truly quirky is our inconsistent attitude regarding our physical attributes. Consider nostrils and ear canals, blood and tears and white blood cells, stomach rumbling and belches. Or hair follicles. Even that innocuous shoulder blade. How'd they get off so easy, I wonder?

It should work, though, all things being equal, calling someone a kneecap or aorta when you're cut off in traffic, or yelling "ear wax!" when you drop a screw into the distributor. But it doesn't, because we haven't agreed that those things are offensive. All things aren't equal. Imagine the interesting and refreshing change in our conversations if they were.

###

July 27, 1990

Classic Comics Bibles

A T A FUNERAL a while ago, the clergyman stood and announced he would read the 23rd Psalm. Good, I thought. I love the 23rd Psalm. He did mention his source, one of the newer translations of the Bible, but I hardly thought that would matter.

Big surprise. What came out of his mouth sounded something like this:

"I need absolutely nothing because God is my best friend. Not only does he help me lie down in the lush green grass, he walks right next to me too, when I hang out by quiet rivers. He makes me feel better. He really shows me how to do things right.

"Even when I think I might die for real, I won't be afraid, because you're there for me, offering me a kind guide and terrific assistance. You feed me even though my enemies are right in front of me. I'm blessed, that's all I can say. Plus, I'll live with you for eternity."

Yow. Any minute, the body would rise in the coffin and scream at him to stop.

What was this? Religions R Us? McChristianity?

My teeth hurt from clenching them. My ears ached from the attack of the awkward words, the sophomoric phrasing. I could hardly stand it.

The 23rd Psalm is beautiful, but what this guy read bore no resemblance to it. It was like having to listen to a novice practice the violin. It'd be more comforting to hear fingernails on a blackboard.

Of course I realize that language isn't static. Things change; the King James version has been around since 1611, for heaven's sake—Shakespeare's time.

My outrage over that shabby translation of the 23rd Psalm is probably nothing compared to the furor raised when the KJV first appeared.

I understand the reason for all these new translations of the Bible. The KJV, you will tell me, is old-fashioned and archaic, incomprehensible to up-and-coming Christians, many of whom, I suppose, want something they can understand *now*. Not only now, but *right now*, something that won't scare them away with exotic words like "thou," "thy," "righteousness" and "anointest," to name four.

These new translations commit other felonies too numerous to mention here, leaden phrasing that grates on the ear. If you can stand it, check out a modernization of the Lord's Prayer sometime. Eek.

In contrast, much of the KJV is beautiful, with majestic language and phrasing. It elegantly presents what the authors felt and knew was itself beautiful, majestic and elegant. How can you attract someone to something you think is beautiful, majestic and elegant with language that is simplistic (not simple, there's a difference), shallow and inadequate? You can't, of course.

I know the editors of these versions want to make Christianity approachable for the "common man," but I imagine a common man probably feels he has enough around him that's common.

Why should he embrace a religion that assaults him with language that insults his intelligence, rather than uplifts and thrills him?

That clergyman who hammered on me with the Classic Comics version of the 23rd Psalm was no kid. He was at least in his 50s. Surely he hadn't been drawn to his religion by hearing those painful words.

He should have known better. Rather than honor me with "Though I walk through the valley of the shadow of death" and "my cup runneth over," he dragged me over the jagged rocks of ugly language. It offered no comfort.

Aug. 24, 1990

Your Bed and the Bill of Rights

N OT UNTIL 1964 did the Supreme Court decide that a married couple could legally purchase birth control. And it wasn't a slam-dunk decision. Some of the justices just couldn't see anything in the Constitution that gave married people the right to decide when or whether to have children, that guaranteed that the State had no business deciding for people whether they would or could purchase contraceptives.

To be honest, I can't see anything in the Constitution, either, about contraception or the right to use it or not to use it. Sure, in the mid-1700s the possibility of its becoming an issue never occurred to the guys arguing about double jeopardy and freedom of speech.

But it just appalls me that birth control for married people would become a subject of legal debate. Married people, mind you, the most white bread and fox trot, innocuous and banal of the millions who might be interested in birth control. I mean, it isn't illegal *anywhere* for married people to sleep together.

Finally, after much haranguing, the Court decided to say OK to those hapless husbands and wives by interpreting the first amendment very broadly. They ruled that birth control came under the guarantee of freedom of assembly. Nice of them.

To some, 1964 might just as well be the Dark Ages. But it

seems awfully recent to me. That such a medieval attitude regarding contraception for *married couples*—sorry, I can't get over it—existed only yesterday just floors me.

But then, I'm lucky. I'm spoiled. We all are. Today's attitudes about contraception bear little resemblance to those at the turn of the century when Margaret Sanger advocated sex education and the use of diaphragms to Brooklyn women.

Opponents insisted she wanted to prevent the birth of more Jews. They painted her as debauched, a lust-crazed fanatic bent on spreading her immoral views. Inevitably and repeatedly, she spent a lot of time in jail. Her opponents growled that disseminating what the law then considered pornography—birth control or information about it—was illegal. They were right. It was.

So what? Sanger didn't care. She just wanted to give married women a rest. She wanted to free them from the specter of another pregnancy that would jeopardize their health and strain an already stretched family budget.

While it's no longer illegal for one woman to tell another about Fallopian tubes, birth control is still a loaded subject. It's so loaded that it seems that those who have the information are afraid to give it to those who don't. As evidence, I quote you a scary, devastating statistic: I recently learned that a quarter of the children in this country are born to single mothers.

I realize that some of those single mothers choose to have children because of biological clocks. Some used birth control correctly but it failed, another complex subject that I don't have space for.

But using my imagination, I expect most of these single mothers either knew nothing about birth control or didn't understand it, and no one took the time to explain it to them. This, in the 1990s, when we have a plethora of birth control choices—among them the pill, diaphragm, IUD, foams, condoms and sterilization.

OK, OK, I'll include abstinence.

It's a loaded subject because of what it implies: the desire for intercourse without the desire for a physical byproduct. Is this wrong? Well, certainly it's unnatural. We're built to have children. But is it wrong? No. I'll say it again: no.

On the other hand—wandering around ignorant and uneducated about one's body and how it works? That's wrong. What's wrong is hoping that those who are naïve stay that way. What's wrong is encouraging that naïveté on an earth that cannot stand many more people.

April 10, 1992

On Browbeating Nonbelievers

TOO MANY CHRISTIANS give their religion a bad name. How sad. The ideas behind Christianity are so uplifting: love, peace, forgiveness, tolerance, compassion, patience. From the outside looking in, it looks to me as if a definition of a Christian is one who not only worships Christ but endeavors to be like him—a man who by all accounts had all those nouns, and then some, hanging on him. Don't we need more people who aspire to have those nouns hanging on them? Of course we do.

But it seems to me that some who profess to be Christian are the ones most lacking in Christlike behavior. They may never covet their neighbors' wives, but they're the ones who throw the first stone. They may never kill anyone or insult their parents, but they're the ones who seem the most intolerant.

They're the ones who, in the guise of speaking for Christ, condemn the sinners in our midst—these so-called Christians insist they're sinners, anyway—and pass judgment on their neighbors.

They're the ones who have no concept of forgiveness, the ones who seem the most narrow-minded.

Even one Christian like this is too many.

This behavior has a significant effect on others. This behavior tends to turn people away from Christianity, rather than lead them toward it. They turn me away, at any rate, and I know I'm not unique.

I'm not searching for a religion. I have a religion. But if I were searching for one, why should I take seriously one represented by someone so hostile? Someone who offends me isn't going to entice me.

The negative-minded disciple who adamantly—and proudly—refuses to consider opposing viewpoints—his attitude is not going to encourage me to bask in the joy of his god's love.

The proselytizer who dismisses ideas if they don't match his own, who judges me before he knows me, or even after he knows me—he has killed his religion for me.

That's what his religion does to him? He can have it, poor guy.

This creates three problems. First, as a result of this acrimony, I'm a lost soul, as far as that believer is concerned. Out in the cold. So aren't I missing great joy and utter salvation? And aren't I damned?

And isn't one of the duties of a Christian to witness for the Lord, bring more disciples into the flock? The antagonistic disciple has driven me away, though, rather than brought me in.

Won't he eventually have to answer for that? What will he say, that I thought I wasn't good enough for that religion? Or will he shrug that, gee, he tried, but I decided that the religion harbored too many small-hearted people? That I decided it seemed specifically designed for small-hearted people?

Oh, yeah? However did I reach those conclusions? It couldn't have anything to do with that angry Christian, could it? Do you think they'll make the connection?

Third, the prickly proselyte does his religion no good by his fury at those who don't believe as he does.

The (surely) inevitable antagonism toward Christianity is a wretched, mean offering to bring to an institution that has given one such joy. Is that any way to express gratitude to the Supreme Being?

Thank you, dear Lord, from whom all blessings flow. Now I'll go out and browbeat some nonbelievers in your name, thus making sure that they'll continue to turn away from you.

Of course, there's hope for these non-Christlike Christians. They do, after all, worship someone with those nifty nouns like patience, love, peace, forgiveness and hanging on him.

Given enough time, the gentleness and tolerance attributed to Christ might eventually rub off. And maybe those other Christians, those who do have those nouns hanging on them, will have a positive effect.

Then those formerly un-Christlike Christians will have some of their own positive nouns to spread around. This will allow them to do their religion and their savior some good, rather than spread the enmity they so enthusiastically keep simmering on the back burner now.

That will really be good news for modern man.

May 7, 1992

FYI: I know, only some Christians browbeat nonbelievers. And I know, it's not only some Christians who browbeat nonbelievers. But, see, I don't know anyone in the Taliban.

The Freedom to Keep Silent

WHAT CUTUPS, THOSE framers of the Bill of Rights. Do you truly suppose they had no idea where their shenanigans would lead? Freedom of speech, freedom of of the press and religion, freedom of assembly... really! They were bright guys. Brilliant, actually. So of course they knew. They must have.

Lesser, subsequent scholars and historians clearly had no idea the practical joke those Constitutional comedians had hatched on the country. And it was the best kind of joke, too. It took a while in the buildup, didn't explode all at once. The best prank sneaks up on you when you least expect it, long after you've forgotten that someone on the sidelines has lit the dynamite fuse.

After 200 years, we're convinced that the First Amendment gives us not just the right, but the obligation to speak. We're convinced that James Madison and his cronies believed in the dignity of everything one might say, write or believe. This has somehow persuaded us that because we have the Constitutional right to speak, whatever we say reeks with nobility.

Balderdash. Being human, Madison probably woke occasionally with a mouth that tasted like a sweaty saddle blanket. Did he feel obligated to inform those around him? Probably not, even though the Constitution gave him that right.

Because why would he bother? And who would care? More importantly, would he seriously urge others to fight for his right to discuss how repulsive his mouth tasted?

Of course not. Not seriously, anyway. That's why his First Amendment joke is so funny.

Madison and his frat brothers must have known that people would eventually misinterpret their enthusiasm. Lo and behold: Everywhere nowadays, people assert the right to discuss the rotten taste in their mouths. Unfortunately, television producers pant to air their stories. Editors plead to print what these self-styled geniuses have to say.

Skinheads' wooly tongues—next on Oprah... The canker sores of mothers who sleep with their daughters' boyfriends—next on Geraldo... The vile breath of sons who kill their parents for money, on Donahue... The impacted wisdom teeth of "Long Island Lolitas" who shoot their boyfriends' wives, on Sally...

So what? Why bother? Who cares?

Yes, the First Amendment gives me the right to take a swipe at Bill Clinton if I want. I can express distrust of the FBI, practice Druidism and attend a Libertarian political convention, if such a thing existed. It also gives me the right to write graceful, eloquent books and nourish others with words as fine as I can write and speak them, to one person or a thousand.

By the same token, it tolerates the existence of a here-today-gone-tomorrow biography of Rush Limbaugh, as well as Howard Stern's autobiography and a shabbily-written exposé on Ted Kennedy. Nothing in the Constitution, unfortunately, prevents producers from insulting me with another in a long line of graceless TV movies, the latest exploiting Tonya Harding.

Bleah. Sure, the Constitution gives people the right to say what they think—that irrepressible jester Madison made sure of that. But nothing in the document obliges me to speak. It just says I can.

The freedom to speak also implies the freedom to be quiet. I can choose to keep things to myself. I wish more people would. Ah. Keeping silent when you might speak… what a compelling thought.

The punch to Madison's crafty practical joke is this: When you give people the right to sound off, eventually they all will. The problem is that many just have nothing to say. And it shows.

Feb. 10, 1994

More Than One Way to Serve

L AST WEEK I heard from a reader who thinks I was wrong to cast aspersions on President Bush's military career. He included an article that he said proved that GWB did, indeed, fulfill his military obligations. Lest I think that he had edited this piece, he included the website he used as his source: gopusa.com.

This reader told me this with no apparent sense of irony. Look at that address: gopusa (as in Grand Old Party, as in Republican). I hope it's not just because I'm not a Republican that I see a problem with blindly trusting a website that heralds itself as GOP USA, with the slogan "bringing the conservative message to America."

Or am I the only one who senses considerable partisanship there? I'd feel the same way about a website that calls itself leftof-center.com, or democratsin05.com or whatever.

Right before this reader signed off, he asked this zinger of a question: "By the way, have you ever served our country in any of the uniformed services?"

That question deserves more than a quick answer, even though, on the surface, he only wanted to know if I'd served in the military.

No. But so what? Here's what I wrote back: "I've never served in the uniformed services, but (a) that doesn't mean I haven't served my country, and (b) that doesn't mean I have no right to take advantage of my First Amendment rights."

Testy, testy. Yes, he got under my skin. I admit it.

But he also made me think, which is always a good thing. So I'm grateful to him for that.

He's not the only one who gives me the impression that you're a slacker if you haven't served in the military, that the military is the only way to serve my country.

Balderdash. That limits the concept of service. I'll be damned if I let anyone say I haven't serve my country.

First, I'm educated. That's a service. And I read. I vote. I give blood, volunteer, recycle. I take care of my health. I pay my taxes. I support the arts. Don and I earn salaries, instead of depending on the government dole. We save money. I refrain from committing felonies. I promote the use of birth control. I expect intelligence from my leaders. I keep asking questions.

And I write this column. That's serving my country. For one thing, it periodically demands we take the First Amendment seriously, proving that Congress has not yet abridged the freedom of speech, or of the press.

Regarding the eloquent, ubiquitous First Amendment: I don't need to remind anyone that its guarantee of freedom of speech applies to everybody. Not just people you agree with. And not just people who have served in a uniform.

###

Oct. 3, 2004

That's Life on the Mississippi

D ON AND I don't travel the same roads. Yes, we put our tires on the same blacktop, but the experiences are different for us. He makes his living designing roads. I don't.

Periodically he'll point out problems with striping or stoplights or barrier rails or even bridge widths, things that I'd never have noticed if he hadn't said something. But as an engineer, he can't look at a road without noticing what needs improvement and what's just fine.

If I knew what to look for, I'd look for it. But I don't have his eyes. I don't know if I want them, because then a ride on a weekend fall afternoon in the mountains would become something serious rather than a jaunt. And I like those jaunts on weekend fall afternoons.

I haven't read Mark Twain's *Life on the Mississippi,* but I've often come across an excerpt from it, in which he discusses what his experience of piloting a riverboat has taken away from him:

"Now when I had mastered the language of this water, and had come to know every trifling feature that bordered the great river as familiarly as I knew the letters of the alphabet, I had made a valuable acquisition. But I had lost something, too. I had lost something which could never be restored to me while I lived. All the grace, the beauty, the poetry, had gone out of the majestic river!"

I recall one of my first lessons regarding the differences of how and what people see. I interviewed a pathologist and observed while he performed an autopsy. It was fascinating. Toward the end, he held out the kidney and told me the man had died of atherosclerosis, obvious from all the glaring white spots on his kidney.

I saw a purple organ. No white spots. But the doctor saw them. He knew what he was looking for, and he knew what a healthy kidney looks like.

I envied his vision. Just as I envied the vision of a tradesman who shook his head at the detailing in a building where I worked. His standards were higher than mine, and higher than the guy who had put the building together.

It's like me with a book. Since I write and teach writing, I read with a writer's eye. So I can't just sink into a book anymore, and it drives me nuts. Either it's beautifully written, and my admiration distracts me, or—more often, to my dismay—I stumble over one wince-producing problem after another.

Right now, for example, I'm in the middle of a fantasy adventure for young adults in which the hero's blood thunders in his ears. Not just once in a while, but every chapter. Or, repeatedly, a chill runs up *and* down his spine. Do you get the idea the author has paid no attention to what he's written? I certainly do.

Or people sit down. Or they stand up. Most of the time, when you sit, you sit down, ain't no other way to do it. And when you stand, you stand up, dagnabbit. Stand. Sit. Anything else is redundant. Most of the time.

The boy also murmurs quietly. Yeah? Quietly? You can't murmur any other way. Try it. See?

Want more? OK, but be careful what you ask for. A while ago I listened to the first CD of an entry in a popular author's popular mystery series. Driving through downtown Auburn at lunchtime, I heard something along the lines of "'Shut up,' I sharply said."

Yow. "Snapped," I screeched. "Snapped! Shut up, I snapped!" I punched off the CD and kept on shrieking. Oh, you should've heard me. My fury didn't surprise me but my decibels did. I was glad the truck's windows were up. Wouldn't want to scare anybody.

See, here's my rant: why say *sharply said* when *snapped* is the perfect word? Doesn't snapped *mean* sharply said? Clearly, she and the publisher figured the book was good enough, it would sell as is, la la la, so why work any harder than necessary?

But I deserve better than just good enough. So do you.

Another rant: if the author is lazy in that example, I'll find laziness elsewhere. What do I want with a lazy author? I want somebody who gives as much a damn as I do about good writing, about a good story told well. I want her to want to take care of me.

I could go on, unfortunately, give you more examples. But I should calm down. And I'd better be careful. If I say too much, I'll ruin the majority of books for you, too.

"And doesn't he sometimes wonder whether he has gained most or lost most by learning his trade?" Mark Twain asks at the end of that passage about vision and the Mississippi River.

Yes.

Jan. 21, 2007

Evidence of a Great Country

TWO THINGS HAPPENED when I meandered outside last Wednesday to get my *Auburn Journal.* First, I peered up at the ponderosa across the street. And there they sat, Sally and Tim Throckmorton.

Have I told you about Sally and Tim? These vultures hang out on the branches in the morning, warming their wings as the sun rises. Sometimes they forego the ponderosa for the snag down below and solemnly stretch their necks, observing me as I pad up and down the driveway.

So it was already a great morning. And then I read the story about Colfax resident Greg Walsh asking the Sheriff's office to investigate whether Obama is really an American citizen. I read the whole thing, from the lede over to page 15 to where Dr. Kirby scoffed at Walsh and his friends.

I don't know if I can tell you how exciting I found the story. You may think I'm being funny. But I'm serious. I found it moving on a number of levels.

Please understand: I don't agree with them. I think it's a dead horse, complaining about whether Obama's really American. They should get over it. He's a citizen. He's the president.

And in my opinion, it's certainly a waste of everyone's time to approach the Sheriff's office about it.

If Mr. Walsh and his compatriots don't want Obama in the White House, they can work to vote him out in November.

But that's what thrilled me. Every four years we have this changing of the guard. If, indeed, we want to change the guard. If the country wants to kick out the president, we kick out the president, and he goes. He goes peacefully.

Don't take my word for it. Article II of the Constitution provides for precisely this situation. Plus I've seen it happen. More than once. Bet you have, too.

Equally as wonderful, nothing dire will happen to Mr. Walsh and his compatriots as a result of their animosity toward and suspicion of the president.

Nobody from the federal government will appear in Colfax bedrooms at 1:37 A.M. next Tuesday and spirit away Mr. Walsh and his compatriots to some secret location from which they'll never return. The Sheriff's office won't drag them off someplace, either.

Mr. Walsh and his colleagues are far-sighted and lucky to live here. Imagine if they lived in China. Brr.

Or Iran or Myanmar. Imagine how quiet they'd have to remain if they felt about their leader there the way they feel about their leader here.

Imagine living in Iraq and calling the newspaper to express your disdain for Jalal Talabani.

Imagine living in North Korea and asking the police to investigate Kim Jong-Un because you believe he's leading the country under false pretenses.

I thought of those possibilities on Wednesday and wanted to congratulate Mr. Walsh and his comrades for their good judgment on choosing to live here.

How wise they are. They can behave in an impolitic manner and I imagine that the worst that will happen is that people will roll their eyes at them. It bodes well for all of us.

And their wisdom must have shown itself many times over the past several years—as when citizens unhappy with George W. Bush and his running of the country made their feelings known. And when citizens appalled at Clinton's randiness went public. Since Mr. Walsh and his compatriots recognize the importance of free speech in a free country, surely they enthusiastically supported their fellow citizens and celebrated their patriotism—even if they haven't always agreed.

What a great country.

###

May 13, 2012

Honoring Banned Books Week

TODAY MARKS THE beginning of the 30th Annual Banned Books Week. Check it out at bannedbooksweek.org.

I love Banned Books Week. Although I hate that books are banned, or challenged, or censored or quietly removed from library shelves, I love that I live in a time and in a country where I can find information about banned and challenged books. I love that I live in a time and in a country where the idea and the act of banning books unnerves and enrages a large number of people.

I understand that certain subjects and certain language offends certain individuals and certain groups. I myself find certain subjects and certain language offensive. But when I stumble across something that offends me, I walk away.

Note, please, that my actions make no demands on you. Whatever I may think, I don't insist that you turn your back on something just because I don't like it. Because this is the United States and we have the First Amendment, I have the right to read or watch or listen to whatever I want, no matter what you might think of it. I have the right to make up my own mind. You have that same right. Neither of us has the right to tell the other what we can or can't read.

The same goes for our children, if we have any. You have the right to decide how or whether to restrict what your child sees or hears or reads.

That's it, though. If you don't want your child to read something, fine. Restrict your child's access to that book. But don't presume to decide for other people's children. Don't tell me, your neighbor, your bookstore, your school or your library that nobody should read it.

That's the battle. It's ongoing and volatile. That's the reason behind Banned Book Week.

I understand the sincerity of those who would prevent libraries or schools from making Atticus Finch, Captain Ahab, Harry Potter or Anne Frank (to name only four examples) available to anyone of any age. Or available at all. I do. Like me, they would prefer a world where uncomfortable subjects, language and situations just didn't exist, so we'd never have to think about them.

But we don't live in a world like that, and there's nothing we can do about it, save behave differently ourselves.

However, we can take these uncomfortable ideas and situations out and look at them and discuss them and work to understand them—instead of trying to hide them or struggling to deny they exist.

As much as we want them not to exist, there they are. And the less we look at them, the less we talk about them, the more fearsome they become. The unknown—it's the thing that scares us the most.

And trying to keep children ignorant of subjects and knowledge of situations tells them something you probably don't want them to understand: there are things we won't discuss; there are things so terrible that we can't talk about them; there are awful things out there that you won't let them learn about.

The thing is, they have to learn about them sometime. If they don't learn about them from you, where will they learn them?

Second, as every generation keeps discovering, making something taboo guarantees instant fascination with whatever you've forbidden. If you want your children to learn something, tell them it's bad for them. Go ahead. Tell 'em it's disgusting and see what happens. I dare you.

Third, and most important: Demanding that everyone turn a blind eye to what offends you makes no sense. It's pointless and shortsighted. It's unpatriotic and the action perfectly defines the word Un-American.

That's why I love Banned Book Week. Because it's so patriotic.

###

Sept. 30, 2012

six

Ms. Mootpoint

A S WITH THE *fictional Rufus T. Firefly, I created the fictional Ms. Mootpoint (a) to have fun, and (b) because I'm lazy. I don't remember anything else about how she came about, except that using this question-and-answer format uses up space. And when a writer's on deadline, she wants to get to the end of the page as quickly as possible.*

While Rufus never deviates from her tone or attitude, I've used Ms. Mootpoint to make several different points over the years. And I can never decide if people write to her in my voice, or if it's my voice in the answer. Maybe it's both. Maybe it's neither.

On the O.J. Verdict

DEAR MS. MOOTPOINT: Here are the facts: Joe is on trial for murdering his ex-wife and her boyfriend. Joe is half Korean and half Dakota Indian and currently married to a Black Muslim woman. His ex-wife was Jewish. The boyfriend was a Portuguese Catholic in this country on a green card.

One of Joe's attorneys is, like him, half Korean. The other two are a widowed white pro-choice woman and a hearing-impaired ex-president of the Sons of Norway who lost his left hand in the Korean War.

The prosecutor, a man of German-Polish extraction, is a twice-divorced father of three, currently married to the Jordanian-American daughter of the local president of the Libertarian Party.

The judge is a married paraplegic vegetarian Mexican-American woman who votes the Democratic ticket.

The jury breaks down like this: two Native Americans (Powhatan and Seminole-Chumash); three Jews; four Baptists; one Buddhist; two homosexuals, one out of the closet, the other a card-carrying member of the ACLU; six blacks; a chiropractor; a member of Amnesty International; one Muslim; a pregnant, twice married, Republican Soroptimist over 30; four retired Teamsters, one blind; a tone-deaf dyslexic recovering alcoholic.

The Filipino-American court clerk once lived in Miami. The

bailiff, a red-haired Vietnam veteran, sports a tattoo of the Harley-Davidson logo on his right biceps and listens to the Grateful Dead.

Considering these demographics, what will the verdict be?—
Clarence Darrow

Dear Clarence: You fool. You can't ask me to predict the guilt or innocence of a person with this paltry information. Nowadays you need more, more, much more. For example, what are the race and the religion of the court stenographer?

And what about the police chief, the lab technicians, the coroner, the mayor of the town where the crime was committed, the 911 operator, the first police officer on the scene, the forensic pathologist, the forensic pathologist's assistant and the forensic pathologist's secretary?

Answer these questions and only then will I be informed enough to answer your question.

Dear Ms. Mootpoint: When a person of one color is accused of killing a person of another color, is it always true that the motive is race? Is it always true that the jury must take the race of both parties into consideration over all other evidence? Is it always true that the jury's verdict should be regarded as the victory of one race over another? Is it always true that the verdict should aggravate any rancor existing between those races? Is it always true that *a* verdict in *a* trial should be extrapolated into a message for the whole of society?—
Salem, Massachusetts

Dear Salem: Listen to the media. Listen to the lawyers. Of course it's true. They wouldn't say it if it weren't.

Dear Ms. Mootpoint: As the O.J. trial® dragged on, you kept saying that you were sick and tired of it. You said that the trial was everywhere, all the time. It was all anyone talked about. Enough is enough, you said, and said you'd be relieved when it was finally over. Let's move on to other things, you said. How do you feel now that the event is over?—**Anybody's Guess**

Dear Guess: Are you kidding? What could be more exciting than reading about, talking about and anticipating the seven movies and the TV sitcom currently in production about the trial? Wesley Snipes will star in one; O.J. himself in another; Spike Lee will direct a third, this one starring Denzel Washington.

And the books! The jury will spit theirs out immediately. Then will come Ito's, plus one each from the lawyers, O.J.'s children, Ron Goldman's father and Nicole's sister—and Kato will bring out a short story.

Of course Knopf will release Mark Fuhrman's *Renegade Cop* while he's on trial for perjury, and we'll get updates on the sorry state of the LAPD, plus the countdown to the firing of Police Chief Willie Williams.

And even as they all make the talk-show circuit, all the lawyers, in particular Johnnie Cochran and Marcia Clark, will be heavily in demand as dinner speakers. Just like Anita Hill after the Clarence Thomas hearings.

Finished with the O.J. trial®? Not for years!

Oct. 5, 1995

FYI: TV ran the damn thing® every day for months.

Same-Sex Marriages and Aliens

DEAR MS MOOTPOINT: I've read a lot recently about states possibly legalizing same-sex marriages. They're close to it now in Hawaii, and they're thinking about it in California and other states. This is just going too far. Homosexuality is disgusting and immoral, and allowing gays to marry denigrates the sanctity of marriage.

Marriage is holy and pure, but allowing homosexuals legal access to the institution makes a mockery of the blessed union of man and woman. It's a slap in the face to millions of husbands and wives. I suppose you'll say that what people do in their own bedrooms is nobody's business, but the whole idea just makes me gag. I can't approve of it.—**Mickey Rooney**

Dear Mickey: Heck, Mick, I didn't hear you complain about the mockery of the blessed union of man and woman when Lisa Marie and Michael Jackson got married. You haven't said a word all through the Charles and Diana fiasco. Roseanne and Tom Arnold's stormy, stupid, ill-advised union raised not a peep out of you.

Well, OK, so you don't want gay marriages because you don't approve, because you're disgusted. If those are your criteria for whether marriages should be legal, I'm willing to go along with you, as long as I get to toss out marriage unions that make me gag, too. If you get to exclude gay marriages, I get to forbid anyone from marrying a professional wrestler. Anyone involved in a talk show can't get married, either. Nor can rap singers who sneer at women—'course, they probably don't want to, but I wouldn't let 'em even if they did.

And as far as my figuring it's nobody's business what people do in their own bedrooms, you're wrong. It isn't nobody's business. It's my business. There's nothing I'm more interested in—especially what you do in yours.

Dear Ms. Mootpoint: That big-eyed, pointy-headed alien who occasionally appears on the cover of Weekly World News shaking hands with politicians—they couldn't print that if it weren't true, could they? My family thinks I've gone 'round the bend, but don't you think aliens are among us, taking over the earth and wrecking our lives—and don't you think these photos are proof?—**Jules Verne**

Dear Jules: Of course not. Rest easy. You have nothing to worry about. If aliens had invaded, we'd know. Evidence would be all around us. Members of each race, for example, would be encouraged to denigrate and distrust all other races, trusting only people who resemble themselves, thus discouraging communication and subverting understanding.

If aliens had invaded, education would be scoffed at, and those who sought higher learning would be looked upon with suspicion rather than admiration. Those who taught would be poorly paid, and calling someone an "intellectual" would be a major insult. In addition, people would look upon the arts as trivial, a luxury, something only liberals think is worth encouraging.

If aliens had invaded, corporations would flourish that poison humans and the environment. Nuclear fission reactors would be considered a reasonable, wise source of clean power.

Aliens would control the courts, which would regularly place children with proven incompetents who despise children. Aliens would control the funding for the child welfare agencies, which of course would conveniently lack the money and the staff to oversee the well being of those children.

If aliens had invaded, a large, well-organized group would work to convince politicians that owning guns has something to do with individual freedom.

See? Pish-posh. No need to worry.

Feb. 1, 1997

Economy, Pledge, Offensiveness

DEAR MS. MOOTPOINT: Hey, how about the managers of these gigantic corporations choosing to fudge their books by billions of dollars? What is it now, WorldCom? And Enron before that? In an absolutely astonishing coincidence, it turns out that Arthur Andersen was the accountant for both firms. You could knock me over with a feather.

This underhanded corporate thievery isn't unusual. Nor is it unusual for the economy to react adversely as a result. Thousands of employees thrown out of work, thousands of stockholders are at risk, and as a result the economy slides. I read a comment from a German businessman the other day who said that the WorldCom debacle just makes it obvious that it's foolhardy to invest in the United States.

I keep waiting for the FBI and the CIA to descend on these CEOs and toss 'em away without benefit of representation, citing the U.S. Patriot Act, HR 3162 that Bush signed last fall.

As defined by this document, they're terrorists. Pure and simple. Section 802, Definition of Domestic Terrorism, defines a terrorist as anyone who has caused "injury to or adverse effects on the United States, its citizens, national security, foreign policy, or economy."

They have to be terrorists. I defy anyone to deny that the actions of these addled CEOs fall under the government's definition of terrorism.**—J. Paul Getty**

Dear Paul: Sorry, pal. Look at that antiterrorism document more carefully. In its infinite wisdom, the Bush administration's definition of terrorism excludes American citizens. So you're free to play havoc with the economy, sell cigarettes to children, force Nevadans to endure 10,000 years of radioactive waste at Yucca Mountain. You can slam the American economy or abuse Americans as much as you want—but only if you're an American. That's probably why the stock market's got the hiccups so often lately.

Dear Ms. Mootpoint: I see where the U.S. Circuit Court of Appeals for the Ninth Circuit says that it's unconstitutional to include "under God" in the Pledge of Allegiance in public schools. I also see that the dialogue about the ruling is about what I'd expect it to be. Everyone—from politicians and pundits to letter-writers and talk-show hosts—screams that the ruling is stupid and blind and traitorous and un-American. The insults I hear are knee-jerk reactions, not thoughtful at all.

I wonder, Ms. Mootpoint, won't we ever be able to have an evenhanded, levelheaded discussion about this decision? Can't otherwise reasonable people talk about this subject calmly and rationally without calling each other names?**—Joseph R. McCarthy**

Dear Joe: What is this, a rhetorical question? A riddle? The answer's obvious. Of course not.

Dear Ms. Mootpoint: A theater company producing *The Hunchback of Notre Dame* in England is identifying Quasimodo as a bellringer, instead of a hunchback—so they won't offend people with hunched backs.

This disturbs me, because they don't go far enough. It's only the title they're changing! Quasimodo's still a hunchback. Worse, he's still deaf and Esmeralda's still a poor Gypsy. And by presenting a play that spotlights Catholics, they're bound to offend Methodists, Muslims, Jews, Mormons, Buddhists and Moonies, just to name a few.

When is this insulting art going to stop? We must work to avoid offending everyone.—**Oscar Wilde**

Dear Oscar: How right you are. We must bend over backward to avoid offending people. A good place to start is the classics, which are in dire need of renovation.

For example, in Dickens' *A Christmas Carol,* we must eliminate the ghosts, because they may frighten children. We must eliminate any mention of turkey, to avoid offending vegetarians. We must eliminate all negative views of hard-working businessmen, so that no one will make fun of them.

And there must be no reference to any religious holiday, so as to avoid offending those who do not celebrate that holiday.

That's a beginning. Granted, it's small, not much, but it's a start toward eliminating all offensive material.

July 4, 2002

Politics and Yellow Ribbons

DEAR MS. MOOTPOINT: I've just turned 18, so I'm new to politics, political parties, and voting. But I'm puzzled, and I hope you can help me. How do I decide which political party to support?—**Citizen Kane**

Dear Kane: You decide by meticulous, long study, weighing the political philosophies, the issues and the platforms. But after you decide, whichever party you support, you must consistently throw all your support toward that party's candidates, no matter what. This is crucial. It cannot matter whether your candidate behaves stupidly or illegally, circumvents the Constitution, kills, encourages others to kill or uses bad intelligence knowingly and without caring.

Once you decide to back a party and a politician, nothing that happens within that party must ever sway you. No matter what. If your candidate appears to make a mistake, you must never concede that it was an error. If you read or hear negative reports about that person, always blame the messenger. Anyone who criticizes a politician belongs to the enemy camp. Everyone knows that. Therefore, nothing they say can be credible.

Once you decide on a political party, you cannot—must not!— let any amount of argument convince you to change your mind, no matter how persuasive.

This is very important. You may hear discussion from some troublemakers to the effect that all politics, all politicians and all political parties are the same. Lies, all lies. The political party and its politicians that you choose to follow—they are different. They are the true Americans.

Above all, know this: The party and the politicians in it matter more than the country they represent.

If you follow this advice, you will never have any problems or concerns with politics or voting. I hope this helps.

Dear Ms. Mootpoint: I keep seeing those yellow "Support Our Troops" ribbons on the backs of cars. Exactly what does this message mean? I think it can be read it two ways. One is a command to those who see it, to do exactly what it says: Support our troops. I also read it as a shorthand statement, implying that "I support our troops." In other words, the person who sports that ribbon supports them. Which interpretation is correct? Or are both correct?—**Tony Orlando**

Dear Tony: There's a third interpretation. I believe you can read "Support Our Troops" as a command not to the driver reading the words, but as a literal command to President Bush. In fact, I think that's the most rational interpretation, since there's actually very little you or I can do to support the troops. However, President Bush can do a great deal. For example, he can raise their pay, raise their pensions and get them home. Be honest: Do we have any actual say over soldiers' pay or their rotation? No.

If President Bush won't bring them home, the least he can do is consistently provide them with more than enough supplies, training and equipment. That's the best way to support our troops.

Dear Ms. Mootpoint: I can't understand the people who don't support President Bush. A lot of their antagonism seems to stem from the court battle after his first election. But that's long over with. They should forget the past and accept that he's president. But no, they keep moaning that he's not "legitimate." The heck with that. And the heck with finding fault with the way the Iraq Occupation is going. He's the president. They should get over it.—**So Puzzled**

Dear Puzzled: Yes. After all, as you say, he is the president, and worthy of our respect and admiration. "Get over it," you suggest. Good advice. Not just for this administration, but for any administration. I assume you agree with me.

So if the country ever elects a president you don't trust or believe doesn't have your best interests at heart, I expect you to ignore your concerns and accept him or her with good grace, stifle your complaints, follow him or her without question or criticism and just get over it.

After all, surely you must have refrained from criticizing Clinton, Carter, Johnson and Kennedy, no matter what they did or how they behaved. Since you're so adamant about never expressing antagonism toward the president.

###

March 27, 2005

Talent vs. Publicity

DEAR MS. MOOTPOINT: I'm about to graduate with honors from Juilliard School of Music. A certified musical genius, I play 17 instruments and have a voice many critics have called "phenomenal" and "exciting." I've received standing ovations at every concert.

Of course you recognize my problem. I can't get any publicity, so nobody will hire me. What can I do, other than continue to hone my talent?—**Van Cliburn**

Dear Van: What a loser. Nobody cares whether you're a genius. Nobody cares about your whoop-de-do 17 instruments. Talent only intimidates people. They resent it. These days skill means nothing in the fame game. The only thing that counts is an overdose of publicity, and the more outlandish, the better.

Get over yourself—geniuses are a dime a dozen! Break through to the other side of the box. Think kinky. Think twisted. Think cracked, weird and shallow, and you may have a chance.

Dear Ms. Mootpoint: I'm a publicity agent just starting out. I don't care who I represent, as long as they make me rich. The problem is, the pool of agents interested in the same thing is already so crowded. How can you help me?—**Ten Percent**

Dear Percent: Watch to see how others do it, and go them one better. Several of the jurors in the Michael Jackson case found agents only after they handed down the verdict. A really good agent would have approached them before the trial began.

Dear Ms. Mootpoint: We once were considered the bad boys and girls of show business. Once, our actions raised eyebrows and made the talk show phones burn up. Sean Penn's with us, as well as Madonna and Sinead O'Connor. We beat up reporters, tore up pictures of the Pope on live TV, dressed provocatively, and thumbed our noses at the people who did us a favor by being so shocked.

Now, though, we can't get arrested. No matter what we do, nobody pays any attention.—**Dead Poets Society**

Dear Poets: Wow. A letter from the Where Are They Now Club. Who'd have thought?

Well, you can certainly take your cue from Michael Jackson. Go nuts. Or do what Tom Cruise does: conveniently fall in "love" just as your new movie is coming out. Share your "passion" on all the talk shows. Then, right after you do get married, hold a press conference instead of going on a honeymoon.

Several of you could claim that you've signed an exclusive media contract with Saddam Hussein, and that one of you is expecting his baby.

But first, lose those wrinkles, or nobody will pay the slightest attention. Even if you suddenly exhibit some talent. For all the good it'll do you.

Dear Ms. Mootpoint: I'm a greatly feared and highly respected terrorist. At least I was once. For years, everyone was talking about me, due to a brilliant and deadly scheme I carried out that killed thousands of people.

But now, in certain circles in your country, the mention of my name only gets you a confused look, or an amused roll of the eyes.

Either they don't remember me, or they don't take me seriously. How can I get respect?—**Osama bin Laden**

Dear Osama: You screwed up, buddy. People have a short attention span. If you aren't in their face every minute, there's too much competition. You waited too long between publicity stunts. I mean, look at your competition: the end of Everybody Loves Raymond, pit bulls and Jeb Bush continuing to go after Terri Schiavo's husband. You have no chance to gain the stature you once had.

Unless that's your real signature and you really are Osama bin Laden. In which case, you should convince Paris Hilton to have your baby.

June 26, 2005

On Modesty and Nonconformity

DEAR MS. MOOTPOINT: As you remember, last Jan.
15, Chesley B. "Sully" Sullenberger III ditched his plane in
the Hudson River. Instantly he was a celebrity. He appeared at Obama's inauguration, spoke with Katie Couric on *60
Minutes* and was the reason for a parade in his hometown of
Danville.

Even so, in spite of the pushy media, at first I had high hopes
for the guy. What with his coworkers, his bosses, his neighbors and
his wife all insisting he was so modest, so self-effacing. He, too,
insisted he was just doing his job. After all, he did skip out on a
Today Show interview.

I'm just an ordinary guy, is what I heard. No, no, don't shine
the spotlight on me, thanks anyway.

Now William Morrow is publishing his autobiography in December. Dang. I was so sure we'd found somebody strong enough
to duck, strong enough to just say no, strong enough to keep his
own word to himself, figuring that he'd had his 15 minutes of fame
there on the Hudson and that was enough. But no, he succumbed
to the greedy demands of the media, allowing himself to become
sucked into the hysteria. He sold out.

Isn't there anyone who can do his best just because he knows
how? Isn't there anyone with the moxie to live outside the clamor?

Does everyone crave accolades, the tinsel and sham of the klieg lights?—**Off the Grid**

Dear Off: I've been thinking about this, too. And at first I was totally on your side, disgusted and disappointed.

But look at it another way. People need heroes, first of all, and they found one in Sully. We can never have enough spotlights on capable people doing their jobs well.

Secondly, he's too much of a gentleman not to do us the favor of telling his story. If we give him the gift of our admiration, I figure that he figures it's only polite for him to give us the gift of his book.

Finally, this is, after all, America. Americans have dismally short memories. It's entirely likely that by December nobody will remember a thing about his action in the jet on the Hudson 11 months before. Eleven months! A year, practically!

Plus, it's a book, not a TV movie; a book, being marketed to a society that increasingly doesn't read. Maybe we'll both get what we want, after all: for Sully to be ignored. Maybe that's his plan. If it is, I imagine it'll work out exactly the way he wants it to.

Dear Ms. Mootpoint: My ancient, old-fashioned parents say tattoos are tacky and ugly and bad, and won't let me get one. But everyone I know has one or is planning to get one. I can't think of any way to prove that I'm an individual without one.

How can I convince my parents to let me get one?—**Trying to Be a Non-Conformist**

Dear Non-Conformist: Well, you can't. So you have two choices. The first is to incur their wrath and go ahead and get tattooed. Go ahead. Be like everyone else. Of course, there'll be nothing original about your having a tattoo, since everyone else has one. Talk about conformity. Yawn.

But there's another choice. If you're convinced you need to prove you're an individual, do something nobody else is doing. Give yourself a Mohawk, but instead of forehead to the nape of your neck, arrange it ear to ear. I've never seen anyone with the guts to do this. Define your own style. I dare you.

Or you could just decide that you don't have to prove you're an individual. Talk about nonconformity!

July 12, 2009

Baffled? Dazed and Confused?
Ms. Mootpoint on Lies in Ads

O*N MAY 16, 2012, the Ninth U.S. Circuit Court of Appeals an-*
nounced that Minute Maid can keep labeling one of its beverages
'Pomegranate Blueberry' even though it contains mostly apple and
grape juices and contains only 0.3 percent pomegranate juice and 0.2 percent
blueberry juice.

Dear Ms. Mootpoint: Please help my family. For generations
we've raised 17 different kinds of fruit on our 100,000-acre ranch.
We have enough labels printed to last us into the next decade. But
now the weather and the economy have caught up with us, and we
only have guavas, papayas and bananas to sell to the juice market.

But what do we do with all the grape juice labels? We can't
print more, we'll go broke. And what do we tell our customers?—
Cesar Chavez

Dear Cesar: You must have a couple of pints of grape juice lying around. Take an eyedropper and pay some flunky to add a drop
to each container and you'll do fine. If customers complain, just
quote the findings of the federal appeals court. It's clear they're on
the side of the merchant, not the consumer. If they don't care
about the consumer, why should you?

Dear Ms. Mootpoint: In these waning days of book publishing, I have to make a living somehow. I've published books on the cheap for years, but now even my cheap system doesn't seem to work anymore. Can you help me?—**Jane Austen**

Dear Jane: Of course. Dredge up the work of a variety of struggling authors, doesn't matter who. The more unknown the better. Gather it all in between some covers. Throw in a story by John Steinbeck and title the book something like "THE BEST SHORT STORIES EVER WRITTEN" or some rubbish like that. On the copyright page you can cite the findings of the Federal Appeals Court. It's clear they're on the side of the merchant, not the consumer. If they don't care about the consumer, why should you?

Dear Ms. Mootpoint: I run a small asphalt business in a small state, and I want to make more money. You say the federal appeals court has let this juice company brag about its Pomegranate and Blueberry juices even though over 99 percent of the product is apple and grape—but I don't sell food. I sell a product with very specific measurements of very specific ingredients. If I don't mix it right, the pavement buckles or cracks or washes away.—**John D. Rockefeller**

Dear John: It doesn't buckle or crack or wash away immediately, does it? People can certainly drive on it for a while. What are you worrying about? Sure, you'll go to court eventually, but you're bound to win any case that comes up. There's a precedent. Just cite the findings of the Federal Appeals Court. It's clear they're on the side of the merchant, not the consumer. If they don't care about the consumer, why should you?

Dear Ms. Mootpoint: Your headline implies that if I'm dazed and confused, I should just come to you for an answer. But now

I'm more confused than ever. According to the appeal written by Judge Scanlon, the court declined to urge the FDA to act. "FDA regulations authorize the name Minute Maid has chosen. For a court to act when the FDA has not… would risk undercutting the FDA's expert judgments and authority."

I get such chills thinking about how little the government cares about the public. But when I come to you for reassurance, you tell me it's hopeless. Yet you almost guarantee that you'll provide a reasonable answer!—**Pollyanna**

Dear Pollyanna: I don't have to give my readers what I promise, even if I promise. The Ninth Circuit Court of Appeals says so. If they don't care about the consumer, why should I?

May 27, 2012

seven

Entropy International

L IKE RUFUS AND Ms. Mootpoint, Entropy International is fictional. However, entropy itself is real. It's a physics term connected to the
second law of thermodynamics. A search for a definition of entropy on the
web comes up with "lack of order or predictability; gradual decline into disor-
der." So because of entropy (because of Entropy), in spite of our best efforts,
c90£w7d∑ c&thh66$p HIT ANY KEY TO CONTINUE

You'll see other fictional immense organizations here, but just think Entropy.

The worse things become, the happier everyone is at Entropy, although the
airlines always lose their luggage, they can never reach a human on the phone
and their banks keep screwing up their IRAs.

As W.B. Yeats wrote in "The Second Coming":
"Things fall apart; the centre cannot hold;
Mere anarchy is loosed upon the world,
The blood-dimmed tide is loosed, and everywhere
The ceremony of innocence is drowned;
The best lack all convictions, while the worst
Are full of passionate intensity."

Doing Wal-Mart One Better

S CENE: THE BOARDROOM of International Corporate Consolidated Gigantic Mart, "The store that serves you best whether you like it or not." Present are the CEO, several vice-presidents and the company's attorneys. Each has a copy of last Saturday's Associated Press story about Wal-Mart's refusal to sell T-shirts with Dennis the Menace's *Margaret, from Hank Ketcham's King Features Syndicate comic strip, proclaiming that "Someday a woman will be president!"*

"Look, what bothers me is that while we're sitting here talking, Wal-Mart's getting all the publicity. We're all for this family values gobbledygook, too, always have been, but this story makes it look like they're the only ones who give a damn. It says they won't sell this T-shirt because it goes against family values. Now that's brilliant. Makes us look like we hate family values."

"I don't get it. 'Someday a woman will be president'—how does that hurt family values?"

"It's simple, Tom. If a woman is president, she's not home raising her children. If a woman is president, she's emasculating her husband—and by extension all men. The family's destroyed."

"Oh, now, come on—"

"Tom, you can't afford to question the validity of family values, or else you sound like a Communist. Or a Nazi. Bad for business, buddy."

"But hold on. The company stopped selling the shirts at the only store that had them after one customer complained. The store sold about 2/3 of its 204 shirts. They ignore the 136 customers who bought the shirts, but take that one person seriously? What if everything offends her, from bananas to poplar trees to the men's underwear section in the Sears catalog? If she thought bubble gum was offensive and undermined family values, would they pull all the gum?"

"Tom, it's family values. You just can't argue in the face of that."

"Joe, have you checked the stores? We don't have anything like those T-shirts on the shelves, right?"

"Oh, no, sir. The minute the story ran I saw to it personally—no T-shirts with subversive messages, nothing promoting the ERA or the women's movement or women in the workplace or any of that anti-family values stuff. You know, messages like 'A woman's place is in the house—and Senate.' None of that liberal trash that threatens the family."

"That's good, but we can't stop there. If we're going to compete with Wal-Mart's family values philosophy, we have to go further. We have to purge the stores of anything that smacks of anti-family propaganda."

"And that's something Wal-Mart hasn't done, sir, even though they say they're for family values."

"What? Could you be more specific?"

"Well, look at the videos they sell. Right along with *Pollyanna* and *The Parent Trap,* they sell *Pretty Woman,* that movie promoting prostitution and sex outside of marriage. They have *Annie Hall,* the story of a man married twice and who lives with a woman who smokes marijuana. I also found *Fried Green Tomatoes,* which glorifies women who want to become independent in their marriages. Plus there's *The Little Mermaid* and *Star Wars,* both encouraging youth to run away from home.

"Worse, the day I was there I found Madonna CDs for sale right out in the open, along with Sinead O'Connor—she's that bald woman who tore up a picture of the Pope on *Saturday Night Live.*"

"I see where you're going with this. Wal-Mart says they're all for family values, but they're not consistent?"

"Right! They also sell birth control pills, contraceptives and condoms. If they're so pro-family, what's that stuff doing on their shelves?"

"Oh, good, good, very good. Now as I see it, our job is to out-Wal-Mart Wal-Mart. We get rid of everything that undermines family values, from career clothes for women, contraceptives, anti-family toys and CDs—"

"We can't forget convenience foods, either, or permanent-press clothes. Those all encourage women to spend time outside the home instead of in the kitchen or the laundry room."

"Have you considered that when we're done we won't have anything to sell?"

"Yeah, but at least we'll be the only store more pro-family than Wal-Mart. And that's how we'll promote ourselves. We can't lose."

Aug. 24, 1995

Annual Report to Stockholders

T HE FAMILY OF Consolidated Gigant-O Products, Inc. has enjoyed four excellent quarters. As our stockholders, you know this, but we are always proud to repeat good news. The reasons behind your hefty dividend checks may not be immediately apparent, so we will depart from our usual habit of beginning with the financial statement and start instead with the revolutionary changes we have made in our marketing strategy.

As you know, name recognition is the most vital aspect of marketing. The product's quality is secondary, if even that important. But most vital is to get that name out there and keep it out there. Thus our success with the recent New Year's college bowl games, with the Car Quest Alamo Bowl, the Tostitos Fiesta Bowl, the FedEx Orange Bowl—and so forth. For the first time, Consolidated Giant-O Products, Inc. sponsored every bowl game on the air.

You also know that there is no such thing as bad publicity. You may worry when friends connect our products with rampant commercialization and complain about the relentless ads. You may also worry when network commentators complain. But recognize this: They know—and repeat—the names of the products. And in the case of those news commentators, they of course work for us. They broadcast the names of the products on our orders.

All that counts is name repetition. This results in name recognition. Thus higher dividends for you.

You know that profits have risen steadily every quarter since we instigated blimp advertising at sporting events. Clearly, audacity and in-your-face promotion work with a captive audience. As a result, we have tested the following programs in many sections of the country:

We have painted product names on road surfaces along heavily traveled commuter routes in Chicago, St. Louis, Houston, Seattle and San Francisco.

We pay metropolitan bridge districts to include our product names on their tollbooths, and to insure that the toll takers wear baseball caps with our logos on them.

We have purchased the name rights to a number of schools and school districts in Nebraska, Montana, South Carolina, Ohio, New Jersey and Oregon. Thus, parents—and more importantly, their children—are daily subjected to such far-reaching marketing concepts as the Champion Spark Plug Joint Elementary School District, the Air Jordan Nike Middle School, Campbell's Soup Unified and the Marlboro Unified High School District. This ensures that the students will grow up with product loyalty.

As we go to press, we are bringing more districts into the Consolidated Gigant-O Products, Inc. family.

We have also entered into negotiations to purchase the rights to rename several West Coast universities. Our attorneys advise us that while we may not identify which schools yet, we can share the future names of some of those schools: Miller Lite A&M, Wal-Mart State University and Old Spice Institute of Technology.

We are proudest, however, of two developments in the works

that are guaranteed to increase dividends and make Consolidated Gigant-O Products, Inc. into an even more demonstrative business force.

One: Since marketing any product involves keeping the name before the public, we have asked ourselves for years how to make sure everyone sees and recognizes our products. TV is good, but strangely enough not everyone watches TV; print media placement is good, but fewer and fewer are reading.

And not everyone attends sporting events.

However, our marketing experts, searching for the activity everyone engages in every day, finally focused on the most captive audience of all.

As of Jan. 1, 1996, we now own all the toilet paper companies in the United States. In March, we will begin to test the effects of toilet paper advertising in select locations. If all goes well, by mid-1997 you will see our ads on toilet paper nationwide.

Secondly: Succumbing to the lure of advertising revenue, the major political parties have agreed to share their names with us. So this summer we'll be treated to the Best Foods Mayonnaise Republican Convention, the Absolut Vodka Democratic Convention and the Stayfree Maxi Pads United We Stand America Convention.

###

Jan. 4, 1996

June's Entropy Meeting Minutes

C OMMITTEE CHAIRPERSONS ATTENDING included Jesse Helms; Phyllis Schlafly; the very pregnant Madonna; Pat Buchanan; Pope John Paul II; and guests, the CEOs of Trojan, Parke-Davis, Bristol-Myers, Ortho, Searle and Wyeth—the country's major contraceptive manufacturers.

Senator Helms again brought up the latest official statistics of poor children: 2,660 children are born into poverty every day. This equals 18,620 every week, 74,480 every month and 970,900 every year.

The committee agreed unanimously that the solution to the problem of nearly 1,000,000 children born annually into squalor is simple: birth control. With contraceptives there's a better than 95% chance that pregnancy will not occur.

Children by choice, children born into families who want them, can afford them and are ready for them—this is the indisputable and desirable consequence of birth control, the committee agreed. Birth control is the obvious, simple answer.

Therefore, Mr. Buchanan said, we must continue our fight against birth control, while excoriating the soaring numbers of single mothers at all economic levels.

He asked the committee to recall if they had heard anyone promoting birth control in the last year or so. No one had. Clearly, every columnist, reporter and network executive we bribed has scrupulously avoided advocating the use of contraception. Great job, he exulted. However, he cautioned, we must continue to discourage and disparage the use of birth control. Make people afraid of the subject, loath to bring it up.

In addition to the usual $450 million given to both the "Parenthood Is Your Inalienable Right" and the "If God Wants Me to Have Another Child, I Will" committees, the "Birth Control Is a Racist Plot by Big Government" subcommittee was voted another $63 million.

All funds are to be used to subsidize speakers and to purchase television time and editorial space to promote the idea that birth control is un-American, anti-life, anti-family and unnatural, and that any organization that promotes its use is a front for sex fiends, satanic cults and abortionists.

There was some dissension on this point. One of the contraceptive executives expressed concern that most people would be bound to see through this idiotic campaign, that it was so absurd as to be laughable.

Mrs. Schlafly, however, told him he was wrong. "They haven't seen through it yet, buddy," she said, emphasizing one of the major tenets of Entropy International: The bigger the lie—and the more often it is repeated—the more readily it's believed.

The Pope added that while promoting the image of "unfortunate poor children" might be great as a political issue, birth control is a disaster. Nobody ever lost votes campaigning to improve children's lives. Poor children make wonderful photo ops and sound bites. But any politician who'd try to make the 5 o'clock news by posing in front of a diaphragm display deserves what he gets.

Birth control offends people. It implies sex without consequences. It's risky. It's terrible politics. Worse, if it's effective, it
means fewer parishioners, fewer consumers and fewer voters.

The contraceptive manufacturers, guests of Entropy, were com-
mended for keeping the prices of their products artificially high, thus
ensuring that poor people can't afford them. The committee voted to
turn over $1 million to each company to compensate for the reduced
income, but the executives refused, saying that it didn't matter. They
made their profits elsewhere by gouging the insurance companies.

Finally, Madonna stood to considerable applause as the woman
most recently responsible for discouraging the use of birth control.
Madonna admitted that she could have used it but, "Heck, I was
just—you know—carried away by the moment. We all do what we
can."

With no further business, the meeting was adjourned.

June 13, 1996

Entropy Takes Aim at Culture

MEMBERS HONORED AT this special Entropy International meeting were President Clinton, Linda Tripp, Monica Lewinsky and two representatives from St. Martin's Press, publisher of *Monica's Story*.

This writer knows she is hired only to record what people say at these meetings. But she feels obligated to report there was a palpable glee at this meeting, an aura of success and self-congratulation that has heretofore been missing at Entropy meetings. This was a different meeting.

Mr. Clinton acknowledged the group's admiration and applause with aplomb, saying only that he had accomplished the job the group had handed him.

In order to refresh everyone's memory, chairperson Ross Perot recalled that job: mainly, to screw up so regularly and consistently as to make it seem as if he had no control over his impulses, to leap enthusiastically from one scandal to another—and anesthetize the American people so that they are now numb to any scandal, wrongdoing or underhanded activity.

This outcome is exactly what Entropy International wants: Now any politician can do anything and nobody will pay attention or care, not even Congress.

The media can shriek all they like, but since they've been

shrieking with no effect for months, no one pays any attention to them anymore, either.

"I don't know why we didn't think of this before," Mr. Perot said. "Well, actually, we did, but we didn't have anybody on the committee who could carry out the job as well as Bill, here. Thanks to him, we can be as power-hungry, venal, depraved or as stupid as we want, with no consequences. Dan Quayle finally has a good chance at the presidency, thanks to Bill."

After the enthusiastic applause died down, Mr. Perot introduced the women who need no introduction, Ms. Tripp and Ms. Lewinsky. He gave them a single plaque, which they will share between them. This award recognizes and thanks the two for "doing their part to convince the American people that women are idiots, they don't belong in leadership roles and they can't be trusted." This, of course, effectively quashes any inroads women may have garnered in business and politics over the last 30 years.

In addition, the group agreed that Monica had single-handedly made the concept of sexual harassment in the workplace a joke; all by herself, she has nullified the progress women have made in trying to convince people to take the idea seriously.

To compensate for the fact that no one will ever hire these women again, Mr. Perot handed them each a check for one billion tax-free dollars.

"This is small thanks for the work you have done for Entropy," he said.

Next, Perot turned to the two men drinking heavily in the corner, the ones representing St. Martin's Press, the publisher responsible for putting out *Monica's Story*.

"We thank you, too, gentlemen," he said, as they stood weaving against one another. "As you know, one of Entropy's stated goals is to hobble culture however and whenever we can, but St. Martin's has gone further than we anticipated. Who would ever have imagined a dignified publisher such as yours would have stooped to give Ms. Lewinsky's story credence? Her story is not worthy of a book and has no business being published. It isn't literature, it's gossip—not only gossip, but old gossip.

"Thank you for doing your part to degrade the publishing business and for continuing to encourage the American public that reading is a waste of time."

"We don't know anything about reading," slurred one of the men—it was hard to tell which one, because of the cheers after his comment—"and we don't care about publishing or the culture. All we care about is the bottom line. What else is there?"

"What else is there?" laughed Mr. Perot, and encouraged everyone to say the answer with him: "Entropy!"

The meeting ended with the traditional pledge: "Things fall apart, the center cannot hold, and Entropy will make sure of it."

March 25, 1999

September's Entropy Meeting

S ENIOR MEMBERS PRESENT included Bruce Willis, Dan Quayle, Bill Gates, Rupert Murdoch, Michael Jackson, Michael Eisner and Thomas Kinkade.

The group spent the first part of the meeting congratulating each other. The organization has made considerable progress, it was agreed, on training the public to become accustomed to being inundated with advertising. The continuing success of background advertising at sporting events was mentioned. It's impossible to view professional basketball, baseball, tennis, golf or baseball games without ads being forced down your throat.

Mr. Quayle indicated that we want people to become accustomed to ad omnipresence, to feel as if it isn't a real sporting event without ads everywhere.

Mr. Kinkade, who received a standing ovation for his success in marketing himself and what has become known as "art," urged the group not to overlook the admirable pervasiveness of ads on the Internet.

Mr. Gates acknowledged the accolades, pointing out that anyone who surfs the Net is a perfect captive viewer; thus we can subject him to the advertising of anyone with the bucks to afford the space.

This gimmick was cleverly built into the system, Mr. Gates said.

People think the Web is unique, cutting edge, he chuckled. It's actually just the same-old, same-old, just another way of selling to the rubes. And the more we can convince people to use it because it's hip, now, cool, the more we'll be riding the gravy train.

In spite of television and the Internet, smirked Bruce Willis, for a while people were still thinking that possibly movies were reasonable entertainment. Granted, he said, movie theaters used to be opulent and comfortable. But that was before we wanted people to stay home. So Entropy had to figure out a way to keep them there, to avoid movie theaters.

Mr. Willis reiterated our plot: subject people to shabby multiplexes rather than plush movie palaces. If the ugliness doesn't turn them off, then subject them to bad, high-priced food, and poorly made, high-priced movies. To keep people at home and glued to their TV sets and the Internet—those fabulous selling machines—make it too expensive and too uncomfortable to do anything else.

The rest of the meeting was devoted to considering the future of Entropy and how to ensure its growth.

Mr. Gates introduced a man who had had a computer chip surgically implanted under his skin so he would know instantly when his computer received email.

The implications were immediately obvious. Today that email-announcing chip, grinned Mr. Gates. Tomorrow, chips forcibly embedded in everyone so that everyone is instantly accessible, instantly reachable.

Pandemonium broke out. While this writer cannot quote people correctly because they spoke so excitedly over one another, the following is the gist of the discussion:

One person brought up the possibility of broadcasting advertising 24 hours a day to everyone. Another discussion focused on the probability of making it illegal to remove a chip from one's body.

A comment was made that if the Texas legislature could make it illegal to publicly disparage beef, if people could be sued in California for bad-mouthing apples, surely we could push this through Congress, stressing the need for a strong economy, therefore the need for a public eager to spend.

Someone else said that people are already accustomed to this ubiquitous lack of privacy—what with pagers, cell phones and answering machines all an accepted part of the landscape. Being instantly accessible is considered part of the good life. As a result, the group agreed, it won't be hard to convince people that being always available is even better.

Since the marketplace is all that matters, said Mr. Gates, this organization must continue to spread the notion that privacy and solitude are subversive, and that anyone craving them is a dangerous lunatic. Mr. Murdoch agreed to play up that notion in all future crime stories his papers published.

Following the reciting of Entropy's slogan, "The center cannot hold, and Entropy will make sure of it," the meeting was adjourned.

Sept. 23, 1999

Entropy's Happy July Meeting

"**O**K, WE'RE ALL here. Let it be noted that this is Entropy International's July meeting. I want to start off by saying what a fine job Sam and Janet have accomplished on the trans fat issue. One of our jobs is to scare people, make 'em nervous. You sure did that, promoting the FDA's decision not to ban trans fat because—why was that again, Sam?"

"I love this. Janet thought it up. Because too many foods have it already, and it would be too much trouble to include the levels of trans fat on the packaging, and too risky economically to eliminate them. Ain't that a kick in the head? At the same time, we made sure to broadcast the information that there is no safe level of trans fat in food."

"Sam, let's keep this issue in the foreground, while making sure that the packaging never includes the information."

"Gotcha, boss. Scare 'em while making 'em fatter."

"And of course a fat American is a vulnerable American. We all know that. Vulnerable Americans spend more money, and that's what our economy demands. Bob Wright, NBC's CEO, assures us that the networks will continue to display only dangerously thin women on their new prime time shows this fall. Don't know how these chicks do it without falling over, Bob."

"And you know that's the point, don't you? Their condition is unhealthy and unrealistic, unreachable by the majority of people watching. But if we keep hammering that gaunt is sexy, girls will keep aiming for that goal, not make it, and feel like failures."

"And go out and spend more money. Maybe, dare we hope, they'll feel like such losers they'll fall into bed with anyone who asks."

"Well, that's pretty much predetermined. After all, controlling the media as we do, we push sex without commitment while making sure nobody ever mentions birth control. And all the covers of magazines for teen girls and young women scream about getting guys to go to bed with them. Meanwhile, we've convinced the schools to preach abstinence rather than tell kids what they should know about their bodies. So youngsters too young to have babies will continue to have babies."

"This of course creates a new screwed-up generation."

"And we'll be waiting for them, of course. Them and their money."

"Excellent. OK—let's hear from the rest of you. What about you, Gates?"

"Nothing new, just the same old stuff. The ubiquitous computer and the high use of the Internet continue to serve their purpose: to separate people and get them uncomfortable communicating face to face. This contributes satisfactorily to isolating people, encouraging loneliness. We all know about those studies that prove the importance of human interaction and touching to our physical and mental health. Were just making sure that there's less interaction and less touching.

"Plus we've made great strides in arranging most people's lives so that it's impossible for them to live where they work, forcing them into their cars for hours every week. The consequences are irritation, distress and animosity, all resulting in increased vulnerability."

"Speaking of increased vulnerability, let's give Dick Grasso a chance to talk. You all know the chairman of the New York Stock Exchange."

"Thank you for your generous applause. A volatile stock market is a good thing. It makes people jumpy and uncertain. All these companies run into the ground by people Entropy International has put there—all is happening exactly as we've planned. We want a vulnerable, materialistic population. We don't want a bunch of contented cows just sitting around chewing their cuds, for cripe's sake. Happy people don't spend money. We want people jittery and nervous. This is going perfectly."

"Thanks, Dick. Well, time's about up. Next month, Entropy International's best friend will be here to talk about his brilliant new program, Operation TIPS (Terrorist Information and Prevention System). In August our man in the White House will start recruiting 11 million volunteers in 10 cities. They'll investigate other Americans and report suspicious, ostensibly terrorism-related activity.

"It's a great idea. Hey, if being spied on won't make people feel vulnerable, nothing will."

###

July 25, 2002

Entropy Discourages Voting

"THANK YOU ALL for coming at such short notice. I know you're all busy, what with the election next week, slandering each other on TV and in the newspaper ads, planting stories and hiring people to write letters to the editor complaining about the idiots running for office. You're all doing a great job, just great."

"Speaking for the group, George, we especially value your support. You know that we're working to make people believe that the system is rigged, that politicians are craven and corrupt, and no matter who they vote for, they're bound to get some crook in there who will instantly raise taxes and pay no attention to the saps who put them in office."

"Absolutely, John. In election years anyway, Entropy International wants to convince people that voting is pointless. The more people we encourage to stay home on Election Day, the better for us. Best of all is the governor's race in California, where most people are just disgusted by both the Republican and the Democratic candidates. We're all doing everything we can to encourage people to feel that way, and discourage them from considering the third-party candidates. We never want people to think they have a choice."

"We want people feeling powerless, you mean?"

"And confused, yes, Tom, that's exactly what I mean. We have elections divisions across the country changing the way people vote from election to election. In one county, for example, people vote by filling in circles. In another they poke out chads, while still another has unfathomable voting machines. And they all switch the system for the next election, so that people can't get used to one method. Among all these options there must be a best way to collect the vote. We could even tabulate votes electronically. But no, here we are in the 21st century, and the process is still fraught with confusion."

"It's a great way to keep people away from the polls. And what a great way to make counting the vote itself inefficient and inaccurate. Look at the spectacular results in 2000."

"You bet, Sam. After all, it's to our advantage to ensure that counting votes remains a horrendous process, and we're successful every year. It's thrilling. If people really thought about it, they'd realize that if those of us in power wanted to make it simple to count votes, we would. But that would just encourage people, make them more interested in voting. That's the last thing we want. So we work to distract and exasperate people with irrelevant issues, like the cost of campaigning, the negative tone in the campaigns, and the shabby behavior between candidates whenever two or more condescend to debate."

"Of course, George, there are some people who insist on voting in every election, no matter what we do. Regardless of the confusing ballots, the incomprehensible propositions, the bad publicity we leak regarding the candidates, and all the outraged columnists we pay to complain about the shoddy vote counting process, they keep right on voting. It's astonishing."

"You're right. These oddballs vote in spite of our rumors that all politicians are self-serving liars only willing to serve special interest groups. They vote even though our people currently in office do their damnedest to distance themselves from their constituency. They're the toughest nuts to discourage—the ones who continue to believe that their vote makes a difference. It's just baffling."

"Not to worry, though. Entropy International has been charged with dumbing-down the population. The less educated a person is, the less he reads, and the less involved he is. So he watches more TV, and is subject to the so-called 'news' shows we produce, which help to spread the misinformation about voting."

"I get it. The more powerful Entropy gets, the more people we'll be able to convince that voting is naïve and old-fashioned, an act that has nothing to do with reality. We know that's furthest from the truth. But it's because we know how important voting is that we can't allow the public to realize it. An informed, literate voter is EI's worst enemy."

Nov. 1, 2002

Least Likely to Succeed Award

MEMO: TO ALL corporate, political and media members
FROM: CEO, Entropy International
RE: Congratulations

Ladies and gentlemen, what a terrific year this has been. We're just starting our third quarter, just a tad over halfway through the year, and the chaos you've engendered has been beyond our wildest dreams. I'm impressed. I take my hat off to you. We still have more to do, but you've proven we have the right stuff.

I have a lot to say about the media. In particular, to the authors of these recent books that focus on accusing the media of "left-wing" and "right-wing" slant, each side accusing the other of bias and slander and treason. It's a good thing to work to convince the public that in every situation there's only black or white, nothing in between. That way, people won't look carefully, or think carefully, about a subject or a problem, and will scoff at anyone who does.

And these recent blockbuster movies and books—I'd like to see more of them, and more blockbuster focus on them. I love this information we get plastered all over the media about such and such movie earned so many millions of dollars the first day, making it the biggest single-day moneymaker in history. As if that means anything!

And the jockeying for No. 1 that made the new Harry Potter,

the new Oprah pick and Hillary's new book so entertaining to watch. People want something because others want it. Just because millions want something doesn't mean it's any good. It just means millions want it. We know that, but they don't.

Besides, the intense slavering for some highly touted thing means you've all done your job. These rubes want things because you tell them they do. And if you hadn't pushed it, nobody'd have heard of it. Keep on creating that market, boys, that's what you do best.

Even more impressive, however, is the quality and quantity of the behavior rampant in both houses of Congress. What a mess. What an inspiration! I can't express my admiration enough. You're doing a superb job at clogging up the works, and that's exactly what we're paying you for.

We can see evidence of this terrific job in the "partisan" "battle" "fought" last Friday, July 18 in the hearing room of the Ways and Means Committee between the Republicans and the Democrats. Childish behavior, time-wasting, name-calling! The cops were even called. Wonderful. I don't know who thought of that one, but who- ever it was, excellent. Just exactly the result we at Entropy want in those hallowed halls.

Recall the words of our beloved patron saint, William Butler Yeats: "Things fall apart; the center cannot hold; mere anarchy is loosed upon the world. The best lack all conviction, while the worst are full of passionate intensity." I know you don't need to be re- minded of our intention, but it never hurts to repeat it.

Speaking of falling apart, how about those pros out there in California? Folks, remember that state has the fifth largest economy in the world, and look what's happening to it!

The Democrats fight with the Republicans, the governor fights with the legislature, the state's credit rating goes down the tubes, and they're all breaking the law by refusing to pass a budget. Compromise is a dirty word for these guys. This is a bunch of real experts out there, and we should all take lessons from them.

We should especially respect Gray Davis, who's certainly done his part. Better than we expected, too. Know this, buddy—no matter what happens in this "wink wink, nudge nudge" recall election, there'll always be a place for you at Entropy International.

The U.S. "president" is doing a great job, too, but I mention him so often that I'm sure he'll understand if I just give him a nod and move on. But great job, pal, with that "intelligence" snafu regarding the Iraqis buying uranium. The more you can convince people you have a second-rate mind and you've surrounded yourself with others like you, the better it is for everybody.

More later, but I just wanted to say: You're all my role models! Continue the bedlam as usual.

###

July 24, 2003

Entropy Celebrates Mediocrity

F rom the mid-quarter newsletter of Entropy International:

Colleagues and comrades, congratulations from the board of Entropy International. We congratulate you who have done so much to continue to enthusiastically encourage the promotion of the mediocre, in this country and around the world.

From politics to commerce, entertainment to manufacturing, the worse the quality the better it is for Entropy International.

Some of you missed our spring convention in Washington, D.C., due to the great job accomplished by the mechanics and baggage handlers with causing delays and headaches. Good "work," guys!

It is therefore our distinct honor to reproduce excerpts of the keynote speaker's speech here.

"...But even more than the politicians and entertainers who keep flocking to our 'promote the mediocre' philosophy, we celebrate and thank the manufacturers—all those farsighted, fiscally responsible souls who embrace the tremendously lucrative system of planned obsolescence.

"Without these brilliant CEOs who continue to encourage and demand shoddy workmanship and the early demise of product efficiency, Entropy International would cease to exist...

"From the beginning, it's been the best of all possible worlds, what with all these high-priced products designed to wear out. It's a perfect scenario: make consumers pay through the nose for products they're convinced are high-end but are really only good enough to get by.

"Plus these products they pay so much for are designed to wear out quickly. Once again, it's the delicious idea of promoting the mediocre.

"But the true geniuses are the brilliant thinkers involved with electronics. They took a good idea—design a product to wear out within a certain number of years—and ran with it, revolutionized it, made it their own. When the computer was a novel idea, appliances were expected to last maybe seven to ten years.

"Now, though, these electronics wizards charge consumers an arm and a leg for a computer that will be obsolete in less than two years. If we're lucky, one.

"The marketers work overtime to convince the public that this is reasonable and to be expected. Plus, we're repeatedly told that the computer as it's designed is essential and indispensable—but it's really a mediocre, overpriced product that becomes outdated almost by the time you take it home! Brilliant!

"In fact, the ads and the buzz focus on the newness, the sexiness, the coolness of replacing the old, encouraging the idea that replacing is the hip thing. Who wants a product that came out a year ago when you can throw it away and replace it with the newest model?

"...We're experimenting now on manufacturing CDs, light bulbs, jewelry, mattresses, plumbing fixtures and car batteries that only last a few hours. Why not? Get people used to something and there's no limit what you can push down their throats, especially with dynamite marketing.

"Everyone's on our side with this prospect. This magnificent waste is a win-win situation for everyone: manufacturers, merchants and advertisers. It insures the depletion of natural resources, keeps money in circulation and frustrates the consumer.

"And it guarantees the continued prosperity of Entropy International!"

###

June 12, 2005

Another Fine Mess with Entropy

W ELCOME, COLLEAGUES, TO Entropy International's first general conference of the year. If the printer hadn't jammed up, you'd have your programs elaborating on the magnificent failures we enjoyed in 2007.

We have mostly good news and some bad news to report. First, the good news.

The board expresses gratitude and thanks to all of you for doing your part to ensure that the system continues to succumb to chaos. We're proud of the number of crises we experienced last year. It's been a long time since the conditions came together so perfectly. But coincidence wasn't all of it. The energy you all contributed to the price of gas, the political situation, the economy—well, I take my hat off to you.

First, I congratulate the War on Drugs committee. Their consistent haranguing has continued to keep narcotics in the foreground, attracting massive attention, convincing potential addicts of its rebellious hipness, thus increasing demand.

I'm sure you remember that last year's Afghanistan opium crop was the largest ever. The result will be more addicts, more heartbreak and more violence in our cities. This will lead to a backlog in our courts and overcrowding in our prisons. Entropy International would cease to exist without chaos, and what better way to engender chaos than to create unproductive citizens?

You also couldn't help but notice the delicious subprime mort-gage "problem." The effects of this brilliant scheme will continue to snowball into late 2008, playing havoc with the economy, throwing millions out of work, out of their homes, and ruining neighborhoods. If we play our cards right, we can roll this economic screwup right into a recession.

Speaking of the economy going into the toilet, we also express our admiration to the credit card companies. The latest figures we have are only from 2006, but even that year was glowing: The credit-card companies took in $17 billion that year in interest charges. We see no reason why that figure shouldn't just keep ris-ing. And there are people who say Entropy doesn't exist!

And late in December, almost too late to be included in 2007's successes, the EPA rejected California's request to set higher emis-sions standards for vehicles. This is thrilling—what better way to destroy the environment than to have the Environmental Protection Agency lead the way? Give EPA Administrator Stephen Johnson a warm round of applause. Steve, where are you? There! Great job, man.

In fact, all of you in Washington are doing your part to insure the crippling of society and the economy. In particular, nobody's even remotely interested in working on eliminating the national debt, now at an all-time high of over $9 trillion. Yes, let's give them a round of applause, too. And don't worry, we'll have plenty of time this weekend to focus on the party squabbling and the insults that turn voters off.

Before we break up into groups to brainstorm new ways that

the Republicans and Democrats can offend voters, I do want to focus on some of the bad news. But maybe it's not all bad.

Primarily, we're always seeing letters to newspaper editors expressing gratitude at the kindness of strangers. It isn't good for our organization that strangers return purses and wallets, change tires, offer rides, wash cars, find lost pets, blah blah blah. Entropy depends on people mistrusting and ignoring one another. And the more often people are kind to each other, the harder it becomes for Entropy to survive. And it happens more often than we'd like, in spite of all our efforts.

However, every time one of these letters appears, the writers are always surprised at the kindness of strangers. The message is a good one for us: that you can't trust most people, that most people are vicious and dishonest. We know that the opposite is true, but we can't let that get out. It would be bad for business.

OK, then! Have a good weekend at the conference, everyone, and continue your fine efforts at throwing the world into turmoil. Entropy International depends on you!

Jan. 20, 2008

eight

Humor

TIME FOR LIGHTNESS. *At least, more lightness. Some columns in this section are more amusing than others. But, as I remember, I wrote them all with my tongue firmly in my cheek. And I had a very good time with all of them.*

A Modest (Ecological) Proposal

F OR THE SECOND time in two days, my husband took the hose to the wasps' nest above the front door. The next morning they were back, busily rebuilding *après le deluge*.

Good for them, I thought, impressed, even though I have no interest in a condominium of wasps over my head.

Consider the tenacity, the admirable single-mindedness of those dratted pests. That specific corner of real estate is so desirable that they insist on staying. Our casa is theirs, and we can't do much about it.

Even though we're bigger than they are.

I know my antagonism toward their building without a permit has to do with their massive numbers—not hovering around my door, but in general. If these wasps dive-bombing me were the last 17 in the state, not only would I willingly enter and leave by the back door for six weeks, but naturalists picking eggshells away from hatching condorlets would suddenly have the urge to come photograph the wonder of these final, brave, surviving insects.

As it is, however, I can't get rid of them fast enough.

I'm just like everyone else: The creatures I hate the most are the ones the creatures that have adapted well and flourish lushly. We shake our fists at coyotes, rats, mosquitoes, flies, ants and wasps, as well as star thistle, poison oak, blackberries and dandelions. Not only because they bother us, but because they're so prolific. Although their superior adaptation is impressive, I never hear even a grudging respect for these "weeds."

But take whales—or sea otters, condors, mountain lions or the snail darter, that minnow somewhere in the East. We divert highways and bend over backwards solely for the animals that can't adapt, can't figure out ways of beating the system. The stupid ones, in other words. We spend millions of dollars helping animals that can't figure out how to help themselves.

This of course teaches them nothing.

Meanwhile, the animals we try to thwart are the ones that keep getting stronger precisely because we make things so tough for them. Mosquitoes, for example. Insect repellent now turns away all but the most aggressive, so now we have six-legged Terminators (survival of the fittest, remember) swaggering around the forest rather than the puny hordes of Don Knotts-like bugs of 30 years ago.

They do well in spite of us, which drives us crazy.

But we love the underdog—those wondrous whales, those darling dolphins. Yet we'd feel different if whales had the same adaptation skills as coyotes, or if the number of mountain lions matched the cockroach population.

I have a modest proposal to bring cockroaches and other ubiquitous annoyances to their knees—and rejuvenate the endangered species.

Create a Senate subcommittee to study the behavior patterns of pigeons. Arrest anyone poisoning ants in his kitchen. Make it a crime to harm or disturb a termite. Sink millions of dollars into rat refuges. Erect protective cyclone fences around Canada Geese families. Support sponsors of Save the Coyote Habitat telethons. Ad infinitum.

And those endangered species? Ignore 'em. Jail any graduate student who dares to propose a study of the sex life of the snail darter. Kill all those government grants. Withhold financial assistance to any state that insists on preserving acreage to protect the dwindling bison population. Deny funding to schools in counties that have ordinances protecting the spotted owl.

After 10 years of spoiling those "weeds," we'll have 'em gasping on their knees, begging for mercy.

And after doing without all that special treatment, endangered species will have learned to survive in spite of us.

Can't you just hear the moaning and groaning?

"Walt? *Walt!* Those damn whooping cranes got into the garbage again!"

Sept. 23, 1989

FYI: I take the title from Jonathan Swift's 1729 satirical essay, "A Modest Proposal," in which he suggests that the Irish eat their own children to avoid starving to death. No, no, no, he doesn't mean it.

Me? A Courteous Driver? LOL

S O WHAT IF it's been foggy lately? I should care? I can see fine, there's no reason on God's green earth I should have to turn on my headlights if I don't want to. I turn on my lights when it's dark and not before. You want to make it a law I have to drive with my lights on all the time, so make a law. Then—maybe—I'll turn 'em on in the blamed daytime.

Geez, it's getting so a driver's got no rights at all. First it was seat belts. Then they screamed at me if my kid rode on my lap. And the do-gooders insist we all gotta have insurance. Why do *I* need insurance? It's all those other saps who call themselves drivers, all those old ladies getting in my way. *They* need insurance, not me.

Now I'm getting dirty looks 'cause my lights aren't on in the fog. What, these people got nothing else to worry about? What business is it of anybody's? If they can't see me, it's their fault, not mine. Shouldn't be driving if they can't see me.

I get the same thing when it rains, for cripe's sake. Geez, the whining I hear! Loony stuff like "decreased visibility." Who cares? Like I said, *I* got no problem seeing during the day. Don't know about anybody else. Those pointy-headed sissies—they have a problem and just naturally assume everybody else does, too.

Can't people get it through their heads that the only point of headlights is to see where you're going—*at night?* I know what's cool—and lights in the daytime ain't cool. That's just for wimps.

And it's the wimps who get so red in the face when I don't signal. I don't get it. I mean, the point of signaling is to let people know that this is what I'm doing, right? Look, I'm getting off the freeway, look, I'm changing lanes, look, I'm passing you, look, I'm turning left...

But that's stupid. If they can't see what I'm doing by looking at me, they shouldn't be driving. *So* I change lanes. It's not obvious what I'm doing? Hello? Why should I have to tell 'em twice?

I suppose you're going to rag on me that I'm wrong, that the point of signaling isn't to tell people *this is what I'm doing*—that it's to tell people *this is what I'm going to do*.

Puh-leez. Gimme a break. My plans are none of your business. I don't care what your plans are. Why should you care about mine?

Next you'll say that letting you know what I plan to do is the courteous thing to do. *Not* that wimpy courtesy thing again. People nag that courtesy avoids accidents, that courtesy makes driving easier, that it eliminates problems on the road, blah blah blah.

Nuts. Courtesy's for cowards, for jerks who don't know how to drive. It's just another example of our not being able to make our own decisions, because Big Brother will always be looking over your shoulder telling you how to behave. Thought for sure I could avoid that kind of un-American thinking in my car. Didn't think anyone would have the nerve to tell *me* how to drive.

###

Jan. 31, 1992

A One–Handed Defense of Ego

A N ANNOYED READER, regular but not devoted, has tossed down her gauntlet and challenged me to a duel. Her challenge was her second letter to me.

She wrote to me last year, just outraged, and grumbled that she doesn't want to read about me any more.

She's weary of me, her most recent letter says, a repeat of her last message. My love for myself seems absurd, she says. My column reveals a boastful excess, shown most clearly when the vowel between the second and fourth letter (or, put another way, the letter that comes just before the tenth letter of the alphabet) appears.

After a recent column, she counted the exact number of occurrences when that letter showed up. She found 44. But she had only counted those uppercase ones where they referred to myself—not the lower case letters.

She challenges me: *Can you do what you do and never use that letter?* Not just the one-letter word she so detests, but that one letter? *Bet you can't,* she says. Let's see.

When she wrote to object a year ago, she got a phone call from me to thank her for her frosty letter. Even angry comments are better than vacant apathy—or no readers at all.

She told me she couldn't stand my column. Ego, ego, ego, that's all the column was. No argument from me, then or ever. But why read me at all? She told me she reads the whole paper, and she refused to overlook my column just because she hated me.

A personal column assumes to be exactly that: personal. My subjects have ranged from cancer and love to books, baseball and dopes on the road. That's the *Journal's* agreement: They encourage me to set down whatever reasonable words come to my head.

Authors of columns have large egos, a demand of the job of author. Everyone who's talented has a large ego—or else you'd never know about that talent.

Sans ego, we'd doubt that our thoughts are worth the energy necessary to record them. *Sans* ego, we'd lack the courage to trust our talent.

Heck—some of my columns focus on me, others on my thoughts about a subject; others merely on the subject. But they all resemble one another—one way or another they're all about me.

Hecklers would say that that angry woman got to me, and they'd be correct. Her anger unnerves me, makes me want to placate her, change somehow.

But that's crazy. She may not approve of me, but at least she reads my work. She reacts, responds, *and yet she reads on.* She couldn't do me three greater favors.

These columns, these words, do what they're supposed to: touch people, make them react. That's a writer's job—oops, there's an "i." Drat, there's another—

April 23, 1992

A Basic Truth, Gone

I JUST FOUND out that pi and the square root of two are different numbers. Completely different, I must emphasize. Worlds apart. They don't even know each other. Pi, the ratio of a circumference of a circle to its diameter, is 3.14159. The square root of two is—um—something else. Not only that, but it has no particular name. It's just the square root of two. Dang. I thought its name was pi.

This shakes me. It's as if someone early on had told me orange is green, and now, 30 years later, I find that no, *green* is green. For decades, I'd calmly assumed that pi and square root of two were the same number. I was positive. This knowledge made no difference in how I lived my life, you understand. It was just something I was sure of, a basic truth.

I don't hold much to myself as a certainty when it comes to mathematics. I'm shaky in that area. As if you couldn't tell. So when I find something that I assume is self-evident—a kind of mathematical Bill of Rights—I clutch at it. It doesn't have to make sense.

In the halcyon days before my world came apart, I didn't understand how the square root of two could insinuate itself into so many situations. Why would it pop into equations concerning the volume of a cylinder, for example, or the area of a circle? But it didn't matter, you see. Those much, much brighter than I had already done the work. If they felt the square root of two belonged there, who was I to argue?

Mine not to reason why. Just *believe*. So I did. Crossed my eyes—whoops, I mean closed my eyes—and trusted. And now I learn that I was mistaken. I misunderstood, didn't hear, skipped school the day the subject was covered. Something.

And I learn this by accident. I happened to read that some years ago the Texas legislature voted to round pi off to three. I thought that was pretty funny, since pi times itself was two—pretty hard to round a number like that to three.

Just so happened that my husband (a former math major) sat next to me. What's pi? I asked. He told me.

Dang. A basic truth, gone.

So now what about those other basic truths I've taken for granted all these years? The law of gravity, for example, or the speed of light—186,000 miles per second—or the speed of sound—1000 feet per second.

What if rock 'n roll *isn't* here to stay?

Galileo jolted the world when he peered through his telescope and found four bodies revolving around Jupiter. This meant not everything revolved around the earth. This in turn meant that the earth was not the center of the universe.

Dang. A basic truth, gone.

And later on, much later, the Voyager satellite, that interstellar *paparazzo*, brushed up against Saturn, sending back pictures that stunned the astronomical community.

No mere seven rings here. The astonished scientists counted hundreds. Not only that, but at least one of them was braided, a phenomenon they'd considered impossible.

Dang.

Well, shoot. I can't go around looking askance at everything around me. Finally understanding that pi is not the square root of two hasn't changed the taste of sourdough bread, for example, or the color of aspen leaves in autumn, or the ending of *Casablanca*. Only my perception has changed.

On my refrigerator, for example, I have a list of the three states in which matter can exist: as a solid, liquid or gas. I don't believe this information will suddenly become wrong, that instead of three states we only have two, or those who decide such things missed a couple and we really have seven.

So I'm safe. For the time being, anyway.

Meanwhile, 3.14159 has its own name. Why doesn't the square root of two? Something simple—like Lena, maybe, or Fidel. Or Mr. Rogers.

Nov. 12, 1992

FYI: Oops. While my back was turned, scientists discovered a fourth state of matter: plasma. According to plasmas.org, "Plasma is by far the most common form of matter." Dang.

Blame the Media, Not Me

I'VE HEARD TOO much criticism aimed at the parent of the teenager who lay in the middle of the highway—he'd seen the same thing done in a movie. "He's adventurous, but he's not stupid," his mother said. "He'd never have thought of that on his own."

Good enough. Her boy's not stupid. Leave her alone.

And how *can* some small-minded people insist that the parents take the blame for that young Beavis and Butt-head fan who set fire to his parents' mobile home, killing his 2-year-old sister? The family's upset enough. Besides, Mom and Dad can't be everywhere at once.

We're all intelligent people here. We all agree that the people hollering about Hollywood's responsibility for the hacking and shooting and the foolish behavior nationwide—well, they're right. It's all the media's fault.

It's been a fact of life for decades: People mimic what they see on the screen.

When the extremely popular Clark Gable exposed his extremely popular naked chest beneath his dress shirt in 1933's extremely popular *It Happened One Night,* the nation's underwear companies went into a tailspin. Who needed undershirts? If Gable didn't, nobody did.

Proof: Life imitates art.

And I'll give you more proof, in the form of a lawsuit my family has waged against The Three Stooges for decades. The Howard/Fine estates and their lawyers continually whine that they weren't liable for injuries suffered when I poked my sister's eye out. But it wasn't my fault! I saw Moe do the exact some thing to Curly!

And remember that episode when the three climbed the telephone pole, using five-inch long spikes on their shoes? My attorneys screen a brief scene from that story that always wows the jury: Moe uses his boots to push himself up the pole—by stepping on Larry's face and skewering it with those spikes.

This scene is always good for courtroom fireworks. Screaming their baseless objections, the dunderheaded defense lawyers yowl that The Three Stooges' two-reelers were created for entertainment only, and argue that intelligent viewers know the difference between a story and real life.

Rubbish. That scene is directly responsible for the seven-inch scar down the left side of my face, put there by my brother after we'd watched Larry and Moe shimmy up that pole.

In addition to punitive damages in the nine-figure range, our suit demands the wages I would have earned as a network anchorwoman—plus 50 percent, plus interest. This ugly scar has been the only barrier between me and worldwide fame and success, and The Three Stooges are directly responsible.

One duck of a lawyer told us that he couldn't see how we could win our case, insisting that the judge should dismiss the case as ludicrous.

Ludicrous? Look at my face!

Over the years people have had the gall to suggest that The Three Stooges are not liable for our injuries. Give me a break. Others, idiots with the brass to masquerade as experts, have declared that I'm responsible for poking out my sister's eye; and my brother's responsible for my life-altering scar.

These intellectual midgets go even further, insisting that my parents should have kept a close eye on our entertainment choices, discussing the events within them with their children—and even turned off the TV if things seemed to be getting out of hand.

Turn off the TV! Now isn't that hilarious? Such horse-and-buggy thinking went out with Howdy Doody.

To my family's great relief, an end to our lawsuit seems near. Judging by the fracas over network sanctions and guidelines for violence in the media, few intelligent people these days subscribe to the obsolete notion that people are responsible for their actions. The Howards and the Fines, in the face of these attitudes so damning to their case, will undoubtedly cave in.

If they don't, I'll just send my attorneys the video of *Texas Chainsaw Massacre,* a movie that's bound to give them ideas on how to deal effectively with the opposition. Whatever happens, they're sure to get off.

Oct. 28, 1993

FYI: For years, Don has posted a copy of this column on his cubicle wall at work. Every so often coworkers ask if I really have a scar. No. No, I don't.

When the Verdict Comes In

MARCH 9, 1997: "OK, folks, lots to talk about today. O.J.'s jury went into deliberations last night. Who knows how long that'll take, but most experts say they'll acquit him. 'Course they will. I have a lot to say about that, you know I do, but first I want to hear your thoughts.

"Sam from Denver, you're on the air."

"Yeah, something occurred to me the other day. Seems like all these high-profile trials—like the one with the cops who beat up Rodney King—ended up with a riot. People went crazy, lots of fights, arrests, looting, property damage, stuff like that. Even the gays rioted after Dan White was acquitted for killing Harvey Milk in San Francisco. And fans riot after the Super Bowl or the World Series, even when their team wins—"

"What're you saying, there's going to be a riot when the acquittal verdict comes down?"

"Well, I'm just—"

"Sam, Sam, the lights are on but nobody's home, fella. Riots are a guy thing. Men riot, not women, you dweeb. Besides, think about it. Who'll be upset when O.J. gets off? The chicks, right? Regardless of whether O.J. killed Nichole, it's clear he beat her up. Don't know about you, but I can't see Detroit burning because of some gal being slapped around a little.

"'Course, the ladies might be kind of annoyed at the verdict, but you've never heard of women rioting, have you? Women? Rage isn't a part of their makeup, so to speak. They're not capable of it. Get a grip, man, it ain't gonna happen.

"Women rioting, what a sweet concept. Hello, Jack from Fresno, what's on your mind?"

"Right, I got something to add to what that last caller said. My wife belongs to a pile of women's groups around here, and lately she's been talking in her sleep. Weird stuff about O.J. She almost growls when she says 'acquittal.'

"Once she said something that sounded like 'organize' and 're-venge on 'em all.' And she's been making phone calls and messing around on the Internet, discussing the trial with people—"

"OK, first of all, she's not 'discussing the trial with people.' She's henpartying with the girls. There's a difference, Jack. And if you don't want her on the computer, lock her in the closet. Who wears the pants in your house, anyway?"

"But 'organize'? 'Revenge'?"

"Oh, come on, Jack, affirmative action's gone and made you nuts. You're convinced women have some power in this society. Sure. If they did, you think O.J. could have hit Nichole more than once? Relax, you got nothing to worry about. Hey, Greg from Philadelphia, what's up?"

"Hi, I know I'm coming out of left field, but you know that Greek play, *Lysistrata?*"

"Greg, you're *this* close to cut-off, pal. You know my feeling about intellectuals—"

"Wait, listen—this guy Aristophanes wrote this play in 400

B.C., about women who forced men to stop a 21-year war by refusing to sleep with their husbands."

"So?"

"So the guys stopped fighting so they could get next to their
wives again. The women made a difference."

"Good-bye. What a wimp. He takes this moth-eaten old play by
some grubby foreigner—not even an American playwright!—and
thinks it has some relevance today!

"Well, well, look at what's just come over the wire. The jury's
back, folks. Like the experts predicted, they say O.J.'s not guilty.
Took 'em long enough, but thank God the system works. Now
maybe things can get back to normal around here. Will, in Detroit,
how are you?"

"Fine, but Motown's burnin', man. The women are rioting."

"Say again? Suddenly I've got a bad connection, and there's
some commotion outside. You say the women are—wait, my pro-
ducer says—what, there's more to the wire story? Let's see… riots
in L.A., New York, Chicago and Seattle, fires in Oakland and Dal-
las, radio talk show hosts held hostage in—

"Say, honey, how'd you get in here? Get away from me with
that! Don't you know who I am? Leggo! Hey! You sure are beautiful when you're angry! Ow! Come on, where's your sense of humor? Oof—wow, you really are mad, aren't you?"

March 9, 1995

In the Another Thing® Catalog

A FTER PERUSING THE *Drink Pepsi Get Stuff catalog, the Marlboro Gear Without Limits catalog, the Camel Rockin' Road Trip Catalog and the Winston Select catalog:*

You? You're smart. Street-wise. People see it just by looking at you. You don't have to say a word. It's in your style, your aura. You're a maverick. Unique. Yes, it's clear from how you carry yourself, the clothes you wear, the column you read.

Finally there's a line of merchandise just for you, just because you read And Another Thing, a line designed to make sure that people know exactly the kind of autonomous free-thinker you are. A line of merchandise with its own cool font style describing it. Because you deserve it.

Not available in stores, the SR line is offered especially to you through the Another Thing® catalog, designed for people who know what they want, and know how to get it. Best of all, each item in the catalogue includes the SR or Another Thing® logo on it, so you can flaunt your individuality.

Let's be straightforward with each other. You know what's happening. It's obvious why we're doing this. We'd be remiss if we didn't acknowledge it. If we can convince you that the only way to be cool is to wear stuff with our logo on it—thus advertising for us—we will. And if we can convince you to buy our stuff in order to earn points good toward stuff that advertises our stuff, we will. Why should we discourage you from helping us rake in the dough?

But you don't have to think about that. Just believe that by wearing the Another Thing® line, you'll promote yourself as one cool, independent individual. It will be clear to all just how well you know yourself.

To receive items from the Another Thing® line, collect the distinctive SR logo, found at the end of every And Another Thing column. Then redeem your logos for the items you want. Simple… yet compelling. It's the SR line, as smooth as you are. Can you think of an easier way to prove your independence?

SR543: The free-wheeling sandal, for men or women. Note the smooth lines, the casual strap, the sturdy stitching, the SR imprinted over and over into the leather. The sandal that calls the muses, that proves you're a cool character. Black or khaki. 400 logos.

SR831: This canvas bag has room for your poetry books in their original Farsi, as well as your *New York Times,* your SR laptop (see below) and your bottled water. Perfect for midnight at the espresso house or Burning Man as you pour over the latest *And Another Thing,* convincing others of your intelligence. Note the subtle SR logo. Black, maroon, purple. 220 logos.

SR993: Grab this T-shirt while you can. It's yarn dyed, 100 percent cotton, pre-shrunk. In addition to the distinctive SR logo is the message "It's Another Thing. You wouldn't understand." Make 'em nervous? Sure, but your intelligence does that already. Black, maroon, purple. S, M, L, XL. 107 logos.

SR210: The classic beret. Not for everyone, but perfect for you—you're not for everyone either. Choose from two designs: the familiar SR logo or And Another Thing in its cool font. Black, maroon, purple. 74 logos.

SR441: You know about words. You know how to use them. You know their power. Prove it to the world with this laptop made especially for the SR line. Results in documents lightly embossed with the SR logo. Perfect for that exquisite love sonnet or that crisp and incisive letter to your senator. 7,243 logos.

SR183: You're cool and the world knows it. Emphasize it with these eloquent retro sunglasses. Sleek, matte black metal frame and tortoise-shell colored temples. Classic SR logo etched into upper left corner of left lens. Wear these to hear Stravinsky and you'll leave no doubt about your individuality. 150 logos.

SR771: Here's the black overcoat you've been looking for. Oversized, funky, mysterious, this classic coat is perfect for day and night. It hides you while it makes you stand out from the crowd. But you stand out already. Note the SR logo on the collar. People will recognize your style when you make the scene in this coat. L, XL. Black only. 860 logos.

###

April 18, 1998

A Solemn Call for More Rules

I JUST WANTED to repot my African violet. No big deal. So I trotted out and bought something to prevent transplant shock. I can't remember the name—it was probably something like Vitarootavegamin with Super Xtra B1.

Seemed simple enough. But then I got it home, and I took a closer look at the label.

The attorneys had done their work: *Not to be used for human consumption,* the small-print legalese solemnly admonished me. *To be used on plant material only.*

Uh-huh. Sounds like more than one person ran out of the Jack Daniels' and, really anxious to tie one on, figured geez, might as well rifle through the garden supplies. I can understand that. I've often found a naïve domestic burgundy nestled between the Roundup and the Bug-Getta.

Then, in the directions for use, I found the kicker: *It is a violation of Federal law to use this product in a manner inconsistent with its labeling.*

Well then. I guess, unless I want to risk arrest and serious jail time, I can't pour it over my telephone. Dang. I can't add it to my gas tank. Can't clean my silver with it or bathe my dog in it. If my color printer runs out of cyan, I can't substitute the Vitarootavegamin.

Now some might think the government's sticking its gol' darn nose everywhere. The Feds're getting too big for their britches, telling me what I can and can't do on my own property. Some might think it's time for revolution again; time to tell the government to mind its own blasted business.

But hold on. After lengthy consideration, I think those so-called intrusive laws are a grand idea. We need more protection, not less; more rules, not fewer; more advice, more laws, more guidance, more, more, more—after all, if the government doesn't save us from ourselves, who will?

We need limits. What is not compulsory is forbidden—what is not forbidden is compulsory. Sure. That makes things simple. That puts clear lines in the sand.

So we need dire warnings and figurative stern finger-shaking on everything, just like on aspirin bottles, cigarette packages, couch cushions, plastic bags and canned whipped cream.

I mean, why stop with my innocuous Vitarootavegamin with Super Xtra B1? It should be against federal law to use *any* product in a manner inconsistent with its labeling.

Consider the appalling ways in which one could misuse the following products: iced tea mix, popcorn, shoe laces, felt pens, staplers, yarn, glue, U.S. Army surplus blankets, fettuccine, can openers, hydraulic jacks, vacuum cleaner bags... oh, heavens, I could go on and on.

You could use that skein of purple mohair as filler for your meatloaf. Don't snicker. You could! Without a stern warning on the label—or in the recipe—what's to prevent you?

You could use shoelaces as head gaskets, write letters on vacuum cleaner bags or glue popcorn, felt pens and hydraulic jacks together and use the resulting mess as paving material.

Stop me before I pave again!

And of course it goes without saying that until they tell us not to, it's the fault of the manufacturer if we misuse the product, no matter how ludicrously. If I scorch my hand on the red-hot burner, G.E.'s to blame, not me, because nothing on the stove tells me I could barbecue myself. If I scrape my shins on the coffee table because I turned out the lights and couldn't see it, whose fault is that?

I ask you: Does it say anywhere—*anywhere*—in the literature for your new car that you shouldn't ram into your porch at 83 m.p.h.?

###

March 9, 2000

Annoy Them and They Will Come

L ADIES AND GENTLEMEN! Welcome to Susan Rushton's fabulous *And Another Thing* column. Susan Rushton's fabulous *And Another Thing* column is renowned throughout the world as the most incredible concept in columns the human eye has ever seen or the human brain has ever conceived.

Of course you know this already, having responded to Susan Rushton's fabulous *And Another Thing* publicity machine that has purchased millions of dollars of advertising on TV, magazine and movie promos to convince you of the incredible quality of Susan Rushton's fabulous *And Another Thing* column. By now you're convinced that you cannot be happy unless you submit to our stunningly effective advertising campaign and read Susan Rushton's fabulous *And Another Thing* column.

Since you've coughed up so much money for the privilege of reading Susan Rushton's fabulous *And Another Thing* column, we know you want to get your money's worth. So we can blather on as long as we want.

You're a captive audience. And since research shows that if advertising hyperbole convinces you beforehand of the quality of a thing, you'll believe it has quality no matter what your eyes tell you. So it doesn't matter what you read or see here, as long as we continue to bombard you with superlatives. If we continue shouting that Susan Rushton's fabulous *And Another Thing* column is absolutely the most fabulous column you've ever read, you'll stay put so as not to miss anything.

Although you might want to start reading the fabulous column now, you might also want to know what makes Susan Rushton's fabulous *And Another Thing* column so fabulous. Specific examples, that's what. And prepositions, verb tenses, adjectives and direct objects. But not just ordinary direct objects. These are special direct objects flown in from the South of France.

We guarantee that when better columns are written, Susan Rushton will write them.

And now, for your reading pleasure, Susan Rushton's fabulous *And Another Thing* column!

I recently talked with a friend about the concept of annoying one's customers. Why, he asked, would you treat a captive audience (like those in a movie theater or an airplane) like dirt, subject them to your grating commercials, just because they can't leave?

I told him that it's probably been well documented that people remember the name of a product if it's stupid, if the method of telling them about it irks them or if the product or a facsimile of it is in front of them all the time.

Of course we agreed that annoying one's customers is a terrible way to treat them. But it makes great sense if it works, if all you care about is the bottom line.

This attitude—annoy them and they will come—makes being a customer tedious and disagreeable. For example, Don and I recently shopped for a VCR. We wandered into a couple of places in Sacramento, ponderous electronics emporiums whose names are well known to you because they've shelled out so many bucks to make sure of it.

Well, sure, they had a profusion of goodies. But nobody could answer our questions. Nobody understood how to use the equipment. These companies have budgeted all their money toward advertising. None of it into training or service. They throw these minimum-wage part-timers onto the showroom floor and figure they've done enough.

The marketing wizards convince the CEOs that once they lure us in with their platinum-plated advertising campaigns, they have us in their clutches. We have to buy. We can't stop ourselves.

Well, I'm thrilled to be able to tell you that **Thank you, ladies and gentlemen, for reading Susan Rushton's fabulous** *And Another Thing* **column today.**

We loudly interrupt the end of the column like this because research shows that only 7.53 percent of readers pay attention to the final few inches of a column anyway. The rest of you are busy fishing around for your coats while the credits run.

So we'll take this opportunity to encourage you to stop by the souvenir stand to buy your fabulous *And Another Thing* **T-shirts, coffee mugs, baseball caps, stained glass windows and power mowers—and remember, when better columns are written, Susan Rushton will write them.**

April 20, 2000

Forced to Buy a New One

"LET'S GET THIS straight, now, we want to do things right the first time. Joe, you got the tape going? Good. Your name again, for the record?"

"I told you, it's Susan Rushton, but I don't—"

"Just answer the question. We don't want to be here any longer than we have to. It'll take long enough as it is, with all the complaints we have against you."

"Nothing I've done warrants this harassment!"

"That's what they all say, ma'am. But you admit, don't you, to owning a paint-spattered, red metal stool at least 30 years old that you keep in your kitchen?"

"I have an old stool, yes—"

"And you got it from—what's it say, Simpson?"

"Her father-in-law gave to her and her husband, Sarge."

"You toss me in a cell because Don's dad gave us a stool?"

"We know about that stool, Mrs. Rushton, because we've had you under surveillance a long time. You and other mavericks who need to change your attitude for the fiscal health and security of this country. The legislators, finally, are starting to see it our way, and are enacting more laws to enable us to crack down on you wrongheaded, subversive—"

"I'm in a cell because of that stool?"

"It's shabby, Mrs. Rushton. It's old. You shouldn't have kept it. You should've thrown it away and bought a new one. Here, take a look at these bright, colorful ads for some dandy furniture sales."

"I don't need a new one. The old one's just fine."

"It may be just fine, but it's not new. What if everyone were as miserly it as you, as selfish? What do you think would happen to this incredibly robust economy? You can easily afford $40 to $100 for a new stool. Anyone else in your position would. Don't bother to deny it, we have constant access to your bank balance. And since you can afford it, you have a responsibility to the country to spend that money."

"A resp—spend money even if I don't want to?"

"Ah, that's the point, Mrs. Rushton. You should want to. That's why you're here, so you'll come to see it from our point of view. There are an awful lot of merchants out there, big merchants, too, with the clout and the funding to influence politicians. They have spent a lot of money to convince you that you must have more, buy more, want more. Your legislators don't want you to disappoint them. That's where we come in. Now, moving on to exhibit number two, the iron—"

"You're saying I should've bought a new iron when—"

"The cord frayed. It caught fire. It was obsolete, Mrs. Rushton. Time to get a new one. What could it cost—$35? $45? You can afford to buy a new iron, for heaven sakes. But no, you had your husband—"

"Sure! I asked Don to fix it because he could! Why pay 40 bucks for a new iron when we can get a new cord and plug for two dollars?"

"Because that iron is 33 years old! You can afford a new one!"

"Damn it, I don't want a new one!"

"What you want makes no difference, Mrs. Rushton. How many times must we reiterate that? The economy comes first, the merchant comes first. Not to mention the jobs of the people who put that iron together. What happens to those jobs if people like you selfishly keep using antiquated items they can easily replace?"

"That's not my responsibility—"

"Of course it is! You're lagging far behind the average citizen here, and you need to change your habits. One credit card? Come now! And—yes, Simpson?"

"Um, Sarge, the lieutenant says they're ready for you upstairs, says to let her go, we have bigger fish to fry."

"Thanks, Simpson. Okay, Mrs. Rushton, we're releasing you. For the time being. But know that we're watching you. Lucky for you, we have to attend a meeting designed to deal with an even bigger menace, a group of conspirators far more dangerous to the economy because they're well-organized: fans of garage sales. Good day, ma'am."

Aug. 10, 2000

FYI: As of this editing, 12 years later, I still haven't replaced that iron. I feel pretty smug about it, too. However, the stool now resides out of sight in the garage. It really is a mess.

nine

Politics

ELL... IF YOU *vote the party line (any party line), just skip this section. Don't say I didn't warn you.*

A Sane Response to Lunacy

THE ENERGY DEPARTMENT reveals that from the 1950s into the 1970s, nearly 1,000 people, mostly minorities, pregnant women and children, were subjected to radiation experiments without their consent or knowledge. Hospital patients were injected with plutonium. Retarded children were fed radioactive calcium and iron. Babies were injected with radioactive iodine.

I heard the story about radioactive iodine on the radio so early in the morning I was sure I'd dreamed it when I recalled it later. That's the stuff you see in third-rate drive-in schlock and find in potboiler spy novels.

But, no. My government sanctioned these squeeze-'em-here-and-see-what-happens experiments on its citizens.

I try hard to look at the situation objectively. There are reasons for everything, I tell myself. Remember the times.

Besides, the experiments have stopped. Besides, consider the positive aspects of big government—it's responsible for OSHA. It informs me of the dangers of smoking. It puts limits on engine emissions so I breathe clean air. Cleaner, anyway.

That doesn't work, though. Objectivity's impossible for me here. So I strain for an indifferent shrug and an I-told-you-so attitude of hey, well, sure, what do you expect? Big Brother, Big Government. Laws, accountability and reasonable behavior are for the little guy.

After all, I remember how the government funded and sanctioned the Tuskegee University study on black men with syphilis, conducted for over 40 years within this supposedly enlightened century.

Treat them? Oh, what for? Heck, they're only blacks. Let's just observe and take copious notes as they rot, go blind, go insane.

I guess I shouldn't be surprised. I'm looking at a track record here.

But I can't help it. I'm horrified.

The thing that scares me most is the probability of other appalling experiments currently ongoing that I don't know about.

I have no evidence that I'm not now a subject of these experiments. And I don't know that I won't be a subject at some future time. The mindset responsible for these experiments still exists.

I keep hearing a rumor circulating about AIDS—some minority groups believe it's a genocidal plot devised by the government. I hear the same rumors about crack and birth control, high-power lines and fluoridation.

I used to dismiss these as crackpot notions put forth by cranks unwilling to take responsibility for their actions. Now I think, why not? Anything's possible. Now I know that even if I watch myself, I'm in grave danger. I live in the belly of the beast, as Che Guevara said.

I can't prevent these atrocities. But I can be better than those who commit them. In the face of immorality, I can act morally. In the face of idiocy, I can behave intelligently. Confronted with insanity, I can counter with sanity.

Will it make a difference if I continue to recycle and give blood, if I seek out those whom I've offended and make amends? Will it make a difference if I resolve problems with care and compassion, rather than fuel them with animosity?

Maybe not.

But maybe it will.

At least the world will be better, not worse, because of my actions. I won't have contributed to the mindset responsible for those callous experiments.

It's not much, but damn—at least it's something.

Jan. 6, 1994

If Voting Were Dangerous

M ANDELA WON. SOUTH Africans voted to kill apartheid. As history was being made halfway across the world,
I stood in front of the grocery store last Saturday, registering people to vote. In the shade the whole time, I was cold. It served
me right, my bare feet in sandals.

When I perform this duty, nobody pays much attention. I'm
invisible until I speak: "Have you registered to vote?" People don't
look at me, really. Rushing by, intent on their shopping list, they see
me out of the corner of their eye and figure I must want something—their signature on a petition, money, something.

So people don't bother me. Registering voters is a peaceful
business. I love standing out there. Most answer yes to my question
"Have you registered?" and smile proudly as they speak. Some just
ignore me.

A few answer no, not yet, and approach me curiously. Like the
18-year-old, this time, who wanted to know how to go about it. So
I handed him a form and for the first time in his life he registered
to vote. Afterwards, I shook his hand and asked him if he didn't
hear those blaring trumpets, too. He grinned self-consciously.

I can't help it. I get such a thrill when that happens. It's a mo-
mentous occasion, registering to vote.

And I love being part of it, in a tiny way responsible.

Of course, it's no secret that not everybody feels the same way. Every time I go out, a few smirk at me and say the same kinds of things I heard last Saturday: "Voting's silly." "Naw—I might vote for the wrong guy." "It doesn't do any good, anyway. You have to have money and power to even run." "I don't vote—I don't approve of it."

Usually, hearing these comments, I let them slide off me. Most of the time, while I don't agree with them, it means nothing to me if they don't want to vote. I might spend a moment trying to figure out how they got to where they are, but that's it. Don't want to vote? OK, more power to me.

But last Saturday, the comment "I don't approve of voting" resonated as I mused on the events occurring at that moment in South Africa.

I have an overly romantic view of voting, a view not based in reality at all. I vote only partly because it's my civic duty and my responsibility. I also vote because it's fun and I like doing it, and because I figure I owe it to all the women who came before me who couldn't vote.

But what if voting had nothing to do with romance or fun? What if it were smeared with risk and real danger? It sure wasn't romantic in South Africa, was it, with all those bombings and rebels taking potshots at people registering the black population. What if voting were a matter of life and death: guaranteed life if you didn't vote, probable death if you did? Would I vote? It's easy to vote when it's easy to vote.

If registering people were a courageous, reckless act, likely to attract carloads of mercenaries, would I still stand exposed and conspicuous in front of the grocery store next to a sign explaining my purpose? What I was doing was easy, my cold feet my only discomfort. Would I do this as casually in South Africa?

And these people who won't vote? What if voting were an act fraught with subversion and revolution? What if it were made as difficult as possible? What if the rumor went around that if you tried to vote you'd be shot? Would these slackers still dismiss voting with such indifference?

Suddenly every reason people gave me for not voting took on a different sheen when I put it against the backdrop of South Africa.

"I don't approve of voting." Uh-huh. Yet what if their vote could abolish the poisonous system of apartheid?

"Voting's silly." Those people who voted legally for the first time, the first of their color in a century to vote—would you call them silly? How about the ones who died because they tried to exercise their rights?

"It doesn't do any good, anyway." I dare the man who said this to me to say it to Nelson Mandela.

Maybe I'm naïve, maybe I'm a tool of the ruling class, maybe by voting I'm just egging on the wrong people... but probably not. I figure the fuss I can make by voting is greater than the fuss I'd make by not voting.

Besides, it's so simple. And even better, I follow in the footsteps of great people.

April 3, 1994

The Thrill of the Campaign!

MAN, I'D LOVE to be a candidate for president. Not the president, of course. What a wretched job. Who in his right mind really wants to run this country? But a presidential candidate just has to figure out what people want to hear and tell it to them. Nobody—even people ready and eager and hoping to vote for a candidate—expects anything but frothy generalizations from you.

A presidential candidate can promise anything he wants. Forget having to back up your statements with facts or specific examples. You don't even have to make sense. Just pander to people's deepest fears and prejudices and massage their egos a little. The result? What applause! What encouragement and enthusiasm, what devotion—all yours for so little!

"Ours is the party of hope, and I am the candidate of hope. Can you trust the other party to do what is decent, what is good, what is right for America? We want what you want: strong families, safe children, more jobs and safe communities throughout this country. And we want respect for the flag and freedom for America.

"Does the other party care about the strength of the family? Look at their record! Under their leadership, the family disintegrates. We need a party and a president with heart who is willing to keep American families together, who believe that parents are the mainstay of the American family."

Oh, it'd be so simple, once I got those buzz words down: families, children, future, family, lower crime rate, safe, truth, America, flag, jobs, community, heroes, lower taxes, heart, faith, family, God. Also family.

I'll bet there's some kind of software package sold especially for candidates' speeches at political conventions. You'd just press a button and out would come those soft, smooth, edgeless, pleasing, nothing phrases guaranteed to discourage thought.

With those empty words to back me up, I'd get applause promoting anything: leaf blowers, street maps of downtown Orangevale, pork sausage links, dry fly fishing and shoe laces—even Portuguese-English dictionaries and phosphorus atoms.

Oh, I know. You think I'm nuts. Get riotous applause promoting phosphorous atoms? Why not? Crazier things have happened.

Consider: "I come here tonight to offer hope to the American family. Our children deserve a decent future, and we can only promise them that future with phosphorus atoms. My opponent, not to mention the other party, would scheme to take phosphorus atoms away from you and your families. But with phosphorus atoms, we can have community heroes again, decent people with heroic hearts big enough to be worthy of being called Americans.

"Give the American people phosphorus atoms, and I promise that we will lower the crime rate in this country. We will reduce the deficit while cutting taxes, and phosphorus atoms will help us do that, because the American people deserve the tradition inherent in phosphorus atoms.

"What is the modern American family without phosphorus?

Phosphorus atoms bring us back to what is basic and good in our lives, while reminding families that we need to stay together. With God, the flag and phosphorus on our side, truth will prevail."

You can't tell me this kind of inanity doesn't sound familiar.

But imagine the standing ovations, the roars of approval! The "spontaneous" passionate demonstrations! And once I began insulting my opponent, the networks couldn't get enough of me. I'd soar in the polls.

The stickler would be the landslide of votes I'd be sure to get in November. No problem! Toward the end of the campaign, I'd just bring up the issues—scare 'em—and stop speaking in sound bites—bore 'em.

I'd lose for sure. See? Simple!

Of course, we get what we deserve. Presidential candidates make those hazy, fuzzy-edged speeches for a good reason. They work. Just like selling any product. If these methods weren't successful, they'd try something else. If we wanted them to tell us the truth, they would. Clearly, we don't.

They're just giving us what we want. And what we want is to be pandered to, lied to, massaged and manipulated. If we didn't, we wouldn't keep encouraging them this way.

Would we?

###

Aug. 22, 1996

Scary Halloween Costumes

T O BE HONEST, I only remember two Halloween costumes I wore. When I was five, my mother made identical black and orange clown outfits for my brother and me. And when I was 10 or so, I had this elegant, old-fashioned silver ball gown with a full gauzy skirt from a rummage sale. Wearing that and my mother's old squirrel coat she kept up in the attic, I was Cinderella going to the ball.

I didn't have to explain the clown outfit. In that coat and gown, though, I had to explain to everybody, because people couldn't tell just by looking, and I wanted them to know.

Recently, with the trick-or-treaters who have come eagerly to my door, some costumes have needed more explaining that others. The girl all dressed up in tinfoil? She had to explain she was a Hershey kiss. And I didn't get the costume of the 16-year-old in a dress, because he looked like a girl. Then, laughing a deep guffaw, he poked gleefully at his foam rubber.

But youngsters dressed as Count Dracula and Frankenstein, Barney, ghosts or Teenage Mutant Ninja Turtles—they don't need explaining. They're also not scary. Not to me, anyway, not since I've grown up. It's been decades since I've been scared on Halloween.

I think I'd like a good scare, though. There are characters that would chill my heart, give me goosebumps and make me afraid to go to sleep. Can't you just imagine them coming up to my door and ringing the bell on Halloween? Of course, I wouldn't be able to tell just by looking at them. They'd have to explain themselves.

Here's this kid in Yellowstone t-shirt, sneakers and jeans. He looks so benign. What could be scary about him? But just let him open his mouth: "Trick or treat! I'm old enough to vote but I've never registered. I haven't voted in 25 years, but I always complain about the outcome and those lazy bums in Washington. Do you believe what they're doing to Social Security?"

Here's somebody else in boots, jeans, and I'm the NRA and I Vote t-shirt. She doesn't scare me, either. Then I hear her chilling words: "Trick or treat! I'm a gun owner who resents any outside interference in how I keep my guns inside my own house. I keep seven loaded, unlocked guns around where my kids can get at them, and it's none of anybody's business."

Yow. Now up comes this swaggering eighth-grader, muscular but running to fat, wearing a Raiders football shirt over his shoulder pads. I'm not scared. This is Halloween, and you're supposed to wear a costume.

Then he starts to talk: "Trick or treat! I'm a professional ballplayer who hasn't had to account for my actions off the field since I reached puberty. I can't read because I don't need to. I can't control my temper, but why should I? And if women don't do what I want, I just make 'em. I'm too important to follow the rules. My coach, my fans, my team and my agent tell me so."

I give him a Payday, just to get rid of him.

One after another, costumed horrors approach me: the fanatical evangelical who would deny birth control to anyone for any reason; the elementary school principal who insists his teachers teach only to the standardized test because that's all that counts; a pack of loud, glad-handing kids who throw their candy wrappers in the street and dig holes in my lawn—they tell me they're corporate CEOs mistreating the environment.

And the brawlers in the street: the Palestinian and the Israeli, the Bosnian and the Serb, the North and South Korean. All scary.

Finally this kid strides up, wearing a dark suit and a red power tie. Fifteen or 16 grown-ups huddle by the sidewalk, telling him to stand up, look me in the eye, speak clearly, be polite and say thank you and please and happy Halloween and trick-or-treat. Several carry cameras and yell at him to look, and the flashes go off.

"Trick or treat," he says. "I'm... uh..." Uncertain, he turns toward the huddle.

"You're running for president," hisses one of the adults.

"You'd like to count on her vote," murmurs another.

"Ask if she has a baby you can kiss," a third hollers.

"Shake her hand," comes a command. "Firmly, like we showed you."

He grins, turning back to me. "You scared, lady?"

I nod and shudder. There are few things scarier than a presidential candidate who can't think for himself.

Happy Halloween.

Oct. 26, 2000

Solving the TV Ratings Slump

I N OCTOBER 2000, it was clear that two teams way up there in the Northeast would battle in the World Series. Oh, wonderful. The Northeast, a place nobody else in the country cared about. The sponsors for the series had been lined up for months, the million-dollar contracts nailed down.

All for nothing. They all predicted the bad news even before they saw the figures—the lowest viewership for a World Series in the history of televising the game.

First nobody watched the Olympics. Then the ratings tanked for the networks' fall lineup. Now this. With fortunes teetering on the brink, careers were on the line. Heads rolled, blood spurted. It wasn't pretty.

They had to recoup their losses damn fast. The economy of the country depended on quick action, not to mention the reputations of time-honored advertising firms and the health of the stock market.

Alan Greenspan demanded a meeting with Bill Clinton and the CEOs of General Electric (which owns NBC), Westinghouse (which owns CBS), Time Warner (which owns CNN, WTBS, TNT, *Time Magazine* and *People*), Microsoft (which co-owns MSNBC), Disney (which owns ABC, ESPN and A&E) as well as the CEOs of Chevron, Ford and General Motors.

Not to mention the publishers of the big papers. "We gotta

have them in on this," Greenspan hollered to Bill Gates and the president. "Otherwise they'll screw it up by seriously trying to investigate."

The group offered several ideas, most of them along the lines of staging another tragedy like Columbine or Oklahoma City, maybe an FBI fiasco like Waco or Ruby Ridge, or pay another beloved celebrity to go nuts and appear to kill his wife and then roam the Los Angeles freeways making calls threatening to kill himself.

While everyone agreed each option would attract viewers big time, nobody wanted to annoy the NRA.

They discarded idea after idea: war with China... an alien from Alpha Centauri discovered in New Mexico... a cure for cancer. It was only after Clinton suggested that one of the presidential candidates be caught in bed with a congressional aide that the solution was found.

Another political scandal! But which candidate? It was hard to choose which man to throw to the wolves, because they were so close in the polls.

"So close in the polls?" Gates blurted, his eyes bright with glee. "That's it, gentlemen! We'll create a constitutional crisis! We'll have a virtual tie the night of the election!"

The ratings possibilities of such a scheme were immediately obvious to everyone. Gore and Bush were called away from their campaigning and the idea proposed to them. Old hands at this game, they saw which side their bread was buttered on and agreed immediately.

The longer the group discussed the idea—an election too close to call!—the better it seemed. The media could all have a field day, whipping up viewers and voters into a froth of indignation and uncertainty, demanding a quick answer to who won the election, endlessly interviewing anybody with an opinion. Bush and Gore could add to the fray by posturing, gesticulating, insulting and accusing each other of bringing politics into the election process.

And of course the lawyers could jump in and do their part without even being brought in on the joke.

Of course they had to agree on the design for a confusing ballot, which took a while, as did the decision of which state to make the focus of all the fuss. Greenspan finally convinced everyone that Florida was best. "Most people know where it is," he said, "Not like West Virginia or North Dakota. Plus, only Cubans and old people live there. It'll be a cinch to convince the nation that Florida voters confuse easily."

The group broke into spontaneous applause. Yee-haw! Miller time! A constitutional crisis! What better way to make up for lost advertising revenue! Who cared about those bleak October ratings now?

Nov. 16, 2000

FYI: As a result of the "election too close to call," the TV news channels experienced an unprecedented leap in their viewership.

James Thurber wrote a terrific short story along these lines—"The Greatest Man in the World," a response to the fanatical adoration of Charles Lindbergh after he flew nonstop from New York to Paris. I recommend your digging it up and taking a look. It's wonderful satire and very funny.

Hating a Prize-Winning Photo

I HAD HOPED I'd seen the last of the photograph. I mean, it's been a year since federal agents took Elian Gonzalez from his relatives' Miami home in a pre-dawn raid and turned him over to his father in Cuba. I know they took him because of what I see in that damn photograph: agents in riot gear, one courageously brandishing his weapon at the 6-year-old.

I never wanted to see that photo again. But then last week it won the Pulitzer Prize for Breaking News Photography. Alan Diaz of the Associated Press pocketed $7,500 for it. And to my dismay, I saw it again.

Please don't misunderstand. I'm not passing judgment on what should happen to illegal aliens. I don't care where Elian lives—here or in Cuba. I approve of peaceful civil disobedience, but last year's fracas was a mess on both sides. Everybody involved behaved illegally, violently. You can have them.

But still. I hate that picture. Remember it? I'll describe it for you, beginning with the two armed agents. One stands in the background, in the hall outside what is probably a bedroom. The other, bristling, eyes wide, stands in the center of the photo. Your eyes go to him first. Then you look at what he stares at, and where he points his deadly weapon: to the right, at the open closet door. And to the side, Donato (one of the guys who rescued Elian) holds the weeping boy. Neither is armed.

This photograph scares the hell out of me. Not only because of that agent's gun and his wide eyes. Not only because the message I get is You Can't Hide.

Any skilled photographer will admit that luck has a lot to do with a good picture. The right lighting, being in the right place at the right time—they contribute to a picture that knocks you sideways, the way this one does. Of course, as with everything, experience and talent count. The harder you work, the luckier you are.

So consider Diaz's mysterious luck that morning. That picture didn't just take itself. He had to be there to frame the subject and press the shutter.

You hear me? He had to be there.

Consider where he was. The door to the bedroom is in the background, and the federal agent is between Diaz and the door. Dynamite spot. But why was Diaz there? How did he get so lucky as to catch the agent finding Elian?

The more I look at this photograph, the more I distrust it. Everything about it feels staged.

I believe Diaz entered the room before the agent did. I believe this means that Diaz was there at the invitation of either the Cubans or the Feds.

If the Cubans invited Diaz, we're having our chains yanked. We're being used. The Cubans figured the Feds would invade sooner or later, so they decided to take advantage and use the AP to further their cause: presenting the Government as the Big Bad Wolf.

If, indeed, the cops were surprised to find a camera in their faces, why didn't something happen to the camera in the confusion? Why wasn't it smashed with an errant rifle butt, so that we wouldn't have this evidence of the government at work?

But clearly the camera is in once piece. So is Diaz.

If, instead, the Feds invited Diaz, we're having our chains yanked. We're being used. If they informed him hey, we're going in at such and such a time, take a dynamite picture—ugh. They took advantage of public relations and used the AP to further their cause: the Government as the Big Bad Wolf. This is the way they want us to see them.

The message I get is You Can't Hide. We're the federal government. We're bigger than you, badder than you and you can't stop us. We have the resources to kill a mouse with a tank, and if it pleases us, we'll bring in a tank. Maybe two.

Overkill? So what? You got a problem with that?

Is this the message my government wants to send me? It's the message I receive. Government as steamroller, protecting me from myself, protecting my way of life in spite of myself.

The ends justify the means. Yeah, I know. It's an old story. I just don't like being reminded.

I hate thinking this way. I hate seeing things this way. Believe me, I'd love it if I were wrong. If you can convince me I'm mistaken, I'd be very grateful.

But until then, I sure hope I've seen the last of that photograph.

April 26, 2001

That Government Money

S O WE GOT our tax rebate, our "refund," our "tax relief," our official bribe, our one-time pay raise, our under-the-table wink and a smile, our proof that Mr. Bush is doing his damnedest to keep at least one campaign promise, even though it's fiscally irresponsible. The day after we got it, we opened the Sunday paper and darned if USA Weekend didn't have a jolly cover story on "How Will You Spend Your Tax Refund?"

Blondie and Dagwood Bumstead, those jolly cartoon characters, stood elated in their jolly doorway, the jolly red carpet out for the mailman, a jolly brass band blasting away, and jolly confetti filling the air. I hated the message I got: Mr. and Mrs. America as comic book characters, with comic book minds to match. My husband and I are supposed to go nuts about this refund, be terribly grateful. As if it's going to solve all our problems.

Give me a break. From what I read, this tax refund—resulting in a couple of trillion dollars—comes out of coffers that desperately need it, that are now lower than anyone expected because business is slow. I've heard that the government had to borrow to be able to afford this foolishness.

Tsk. My leaders. Talk about comic book characters.

I mean, come on. Social Security needs shoring up. The national debt needs paying down. Schools need real help. And so the best response these Mortimer Snerds can come up with is *I know! Let's just distract everybody!*

I hate being embarrassed by my government. And my government keeps embarrassing me, thinking up new ways to redden my face before the rest of the world. Kyoto, mines, germ warfare, safety at work, the missing laptops and guns at the FBI. This check is just another embarrassment.

But what I really hate is the weasely spin job on the front of the check. "Tax Relief for America's Workers," it crows. This phrase smacks of public relations committees and oily advertising executives paid to obfuscate, distract and dazzle with the magic act while the hand you can't see performs some nefarious abracadabra.

Tax relief for America's workers? Malarkey. Three hundred to 600 bucks ain't tax relief, and they know it. You want tax relief? Abolish the sales tax—there's tax relief for you. Abolish my property tax. Rehabilitate prisoners so that my tax dollars don't pay to educate felons to be worse felons. Don't tax my interest on my savings account. Or—here's a wild idea—rework the ridiculous, woefully inadequate tax system so that if we have to pay taxes, we're all taxed fairly.

Now, I have a choice about this money, right? Sure, I have several choices. I could, for example, tear it up, showing my contempt for this bribe. Well, yeah, I could. But I won't. I blush to say that. But I'm not going to.

Of course, we could spend it. Yes! I see lots of articles telling people what they can do with their $300 or $600. Travel articles muse how far you can go on the government's dime. The question of the day asks people how they'll spend their tax windfall. Sure!

Spend it! How else will they get back all their dough?

Funny thing. I've seen a lot of articles about what to do with the money. But only once did I see any mention of—forgive the expression—saving it. "Even if you only stick it in the bank," this person wrote, I forget where.

Save it? Saving it *(chuckle! How sweet, how utterly amusing)* is clearly the last option, the thing to do only if you've exhausted every other idea, can't think of a thing to buy, if you have no imagination.

There's nothing sexy or exciting or fun about saving money. Saving money takes patience. It means (oh, ick) delayed gratification, and that's not sexy or exciting, either. You want sexy and exciting? Heck, buy a big-screen TV. Or a DVD player. Or fly to Mazatlan.

Besides (this is the real reason behind that message to SPEND-SPENDSPEND), if you squirrel away your money you do nothing positive for the economy. It goes without saying that the economy takes precedence over whatever selfish, trivial, shortsighted, picayune economic plans you might have.

So of course Don and I stuck our "Tax Relief for America's Workers" away. No better way to express my anger at my leaders than doing the opposite of what they want me to do, caring more about our own fiscal health than the nation's.

Talk about insubordination.

Aug. 23, 2001

The 500-Pound Gorilla

I'M GOING TO make people mad. It doesn't matter, though. I've thought about this subject for weeks, started to write about it several times, and wrote about books instead. Wrote about hair and voting. Because I was a coward. But I don't like feeling huddled and spineless. I don't like the idea that people (you, my government, my president, Canadians, just to name a few) might take my silence for approval.

We're apparently teed off at Saddam Hussein. For good reasons, I acknowledge. I will never say that we should buddy up to a guy who, it seems, threatens world peace, has an itchy trigger finger and can't be trusted around "weapons of mass destruction."

The State Department has lots of evidence against him. Among other things, he has hurt and mistreated his citizens, and has hurt and mistreated the citizens of a neighboring country. And word is that he's close to developing a nuclear bomb.

Terrible, yes. However, let he who is without sin cast the first stone.

We need to clean up our own house before we yell at others to clean up theirs. But we won't. We can do whatever we want. We're the 500-pound gorilla.

According to several Internet sources, among them the National Resources Defense Council, the Coalition to Reduce Nuclear

Dangers and the BBC, the approximate numbers of nuclear weapons stockpiled worldwide break down like this: Russia has 22,500, France has 450, China has 400, the U.K. has 260, and the U.S. has 12,070.

But forget about those numbers and let's just look at ourselves. If it's awful that Saddam might have nuclear capability, why is it OK that we do? Don't tell me we're more dependable than he is. Don't tell me that God's on our side—that's a specious argument. No. If it's not OK for him, it's not OK for us.

And if we're so intent on making Saddam get rid of the one nuclear weapon he might have, why don't we make just as big a fuss about everyone else getting rid of theirs… while we, by the way, get rid of ours? Don't we have a responsibility to at least appear consistent?

Another reason we don't like Saddam: He's mistreated his citizens. Oh, yeah? Well, I've started, I might as well finish. This government of yours ain't no babe in the woods. What your government has chosen to inflict on its own citizens is embarrassing, to say the least. At the most, it's infuriating and criminal.

Consider the Tuskegee syphilis project. For 40 years, from 1932 to 1972, your government's Public Health Service chose to mislead and leave untreated 399 black men in Alabama who were infected with syphilis. The government had medication to treat them, but chose not to use it. As a direct result of this debacle, 128 men died of syphilis or related ailments, at least 40 wives were infected, and 19 children contracted the disease at birth. Nice, huh?

More evidence of your government-sponsored racism: Executive Order 9066, signed by President Franklin D. Roosevelt on Feb.

19, 1942, resulted in the forced evacuation and three-year intern-ment of 110,000 American citizens, citizens whose constitutional rights your government violated for no reason other than that they were of Japanese ancestry.

You'll note that it's taken me this long to get to that Orwellian Homeland Security Bill, which gives your government permission to spy on its own citizens and track our private lives from both gov-ernment and commercial electronic sources. Not to mention the FBI's malevolence. It has the right to spy on your reading habits, and forbids librarians and bookstore owners from telling you whether your privacy has been invaded.

If Saddam should clean up his act, we should do the same. But will we? Fat chance.

Oh, I know, you're going to order me to leave this country if I'm so angry. How dare I write so disrespectfully when we're fight-ing a war on terrorism?

I dare because I think we're better than this. I dare because I deserve to be respected by my government. I dare because I'm a U.S. citizen. I dare because I'm convinced we don't have to strut our stuff everywhere. I dare because I can't believe I'm the only intelligent person who worries about this.

And I dare to speak up because my constitution gives me that right. For the time being.

Nov. 21, 2002

Disappointing and Alarming

PORTIONS OF LETTERS *I expect to receive as the Department of Homeland Security increases its investigative powers, invading my privacy in the guise of protecting me:*

Dear Ms. Rushton: The Department of Energy and your president note with disappointment and alarm that your electricity usage has dipped below baseline for 41 months in a row. This is no way to help the economy. Should you continue this unpatriotic behavior, we will raise the price of your kilowatt-hours, bill you for electricity you don't use or just stop selling you electricity.

Dear Ms. Rushton: The Federal Trade Commission and your president note with disappointment and alarm that you persist in driving automobiles over seven years old. With the variety of options regarding payment schedules, there is no reason for you not to drive new cars, especially the impressive models that insure the continued health of the auto manufacturers and the oil companies by patriotically burning 13 mpg or less. We all have a responsibility to keep the economy healthy.

Dear Ms. Rushton: The Federal Reserve and your president note with disappointment and alarm that for the past 23 years you have paid off the balance of your credit card bill every month. We demand that you max out your credit card and then pay only the monthly minimum. You have 31 days in which to do this; if you do not, we will max it out for you, contributing the money to the Big Tobacco Legal Defense Fund.

Dear Ms. Rushton: The Internal Revenue Service and your president note with disappointment and alarm that the amount in your savings account exceeds the maximum allowable under federal law. Surely you know that saving money is not the American way. Money must circulate. We demand that you reduce the balance of these funds below statutory limits within 63 days, or we will withdraw it for you and turn it over to the Arthur Andersen Legal Defense Fund.

Dear Ms. Rushton: The Federal Communications Commission and your president note with disappointment and alarm that you still don't have a cell phone. A phone bill under $53 a month just won't keep the Phone Company in the black, Ms. Rushton.

Dear Ms. Rushton: The Department of the Treasury and your president note with disappointment and alarm that you often choose to pay for your purchases with cash. Surely you are aware that cash is an old-fashioned, 19th-century method of exchange. Cash is inefficient and spreads disease, and using it gives us no record of the purchases you make. We assume you will alter your unpatriotic habits in the near future.

Dear Ms. Rushton: The Association of Television Broadcasters and your president note with disappointment and alarm that you only have one television in your home, yet two people live there. Are you not aware that the majority of patriotic American households have an average of 1.3 televisions per person? Ms. Rushton, with both of you working, you can afford another TV.

Dear Ms. Rushton: The Department of Justice and your president note with disappointment and alarm that in spite of the highly publicized behavior of unethical government officials and corporate executives, you have chosen to remain out of the legal system. Come, come: We've given you corrupt role models to emulate, we've rewarded illegal behavior, but you clearly haven't gotten the message. The vast legal system—trial attorneys, bail bondsmen, correction officials, the corporations that service correction facilities and the construction companies that build them—depends on the support and participation of all of us, Ms. Rushton.

Dear Ms. Rushton: The Federal Bureau of Investigation and your president note with disappointment and alarm that in spite of the horror stories we've planted in the media surrounding the government's right to spy on your reading habits, you continue to purchase books and patronize your public library. Just as if we weren't spying on you. This won't do. It is not in America's best interests for you to read, yet you continue this unpatriotic practice in spite of our extremely well-publicized discouragement.

How exciting. I can unnerve the powers that be merely by living a quiet and simple life.

Jan. 1, 2003

FYI: I now have a cell phone, and the amount in my savings account has dropped. Is that patriotic, or what?

Me: First Lady for Just One Term

"MA'AM, THE PARTY would like to meet with you to discuss the projects they want you to promote: spelling, dental hygiene, safe roads and—"

"I'm already involved with projects I plan on promoting. I don't have time for more."

"Yes, Ma'am, but the party believes that the projects you're currently involved in are—how shall I say this—inappropriate."

"No, they're not. They're all important: free birth control, recycling, freedom of speech, teaching people how to see the lies in advertising, true prison reform, legalizing hemp growing…"

"But Ma'am, the party believes that you as the First Lady should work on projects that are less visible, less—um—potentially offensive and politically risky."

"I've worked on these projects for decades. The president doesn't object, you haven't objected before now and I have no intention of subverting my involvement just because the party has the mistaken impression that they're offensive."

"Well, that's only part of it. Talking about lies in advertising—that's bad for the economy."

"Yeah? Well, here's a concept. Maybe the advertisers should stop lying."

Later: "Ma'am, the talk shows are complaining that you walk

barefoot around the residence."

"So?"

"They insist you have no right to treat the nation's house that way."

"They'll get over it."

"But, Ma'am, with all due respect, Jackie Kennedy wouldn't have gone around barefoot. Nor would Mamie Eisenhower, or Nancy Reagan, or Barbara Bush."

"I'm not those women. What else?"

"The photographers are here for the photo op of you during your daily hour of privacy."

"They want to take pictures of me alone? That's what you're saying?"

"Well, yes, Ma'am. Since you told that reporter you wanted time alone every day, the media have expressed interest in wanting to know what you do when you're by yourself. We suggested a human-interest story about your requirement for solitude."

"And they want a picture of me by myself. How silly. Tell 'em to forget it. What part of 'leave me alone' don't they understand? They get enough pictures of me."

"But, Ma'am, the public has the right to know what you do when you're by yourself."

"No they don't. When I'm alone, I'm alone. No dopey posed shot of the First Lady By Herself. The idea makes me gag."

Later: "Ma'am, the representatives of the women's shoe companies are here for the meeting. You remember, the one we set up to discuss your only owning one pair each of sandals, black low heels, brown low heels, blue low heels, running shoes and loafers."

"Isn't this the bunch having a hissy fit because they're worried women will stop buying shoes because I wear mine until they fall apart?"

"Yes, Ma'am. The First Lady has traditionally been a fashion role-model."

"Please. If women want to buy shoes, they will. If they don't, they won't. They're free agents."

"Yes, but these representatives are interested in doing for you what Oleg Cassini and Adolfo did for Jackie Kennedy and Nancy Reagan."

"You mean plying me with fancy shoes if I promise to wear them at public events? Lordy. Tell them I'm not interested."

Later: "Ma'am, the media is quoting your husband's opponent in the next election. He's accusing you of being a feminist."

"And your point?"

"Aren't you going to issue a response?"

"'Course not. He's right. Just as he was right when he called me a card-carrying member of the ACLU."

"Forgive me for saying so, but you do understand that the party considers you an Achilles' heel for your husband's potential re-election."

"Well, maybe I'll run instead. That ought to be interesting."

###

June 17, 2004

Pomp and Circumstance

T HE COLUMN THAT follows, with some revision and editing, is a quadrennial event. Something like it first appeared 20
years ago.

Around this time in January, 2005, all of us were counting
down the days until Tuesday, when Washington has a spasm felt
'round the world: another inauguration day, another day of pomp,
circumstance and conspicuous consumption.

Even if you're a Democrat and voted for Obama, you can't
really believe he's the best person for the job. Really? The best person? Did the best person even run?

Voting for president is like flipping a coin or tossing a dart,
blindfolded, at a target. You fervently hope that the winner won't
muck things up. Maybe Mr. Obama should take both the presidential oath as well as the Hippocratic oath, promising to "First, do no
harm."

Granted, presidents are big men, and most of them have been
nice guys, I guess. But it seems that not even the president is im-
mune to the Peter Principle: In every organization, employees rise
to the level of their incompetence—and stay there.

My proof comes from my unhappy observation that for lo
these many years, since before I reached voting age, no president
has refrained from embarrassing me. There has never been a presi-

dent whose warmongering or posturing or idiotic or illegal or deceptive or randy or ignorant behavior has not made me wince with annoyance and frustration, regret and humiliation.

I want a president who doesn't embarrass me in front of the world. I want a president who doesn't do stupid things, say stupid things, believe stupid things.

I want a president who has no need for spin doctors, someone whose actions and statements are reasonable and understandable and therefore don't need explaining. I want a president who doesn't need a pack of sycophants constantly huddling at his ear. I want a president who doesn't need handling.

The president I deserve doesn't hang on his army of advisors to tell him the right thing to do. He doesn't hang on the most recent poll to tell him what to do. He knows the right thing to do and trusts himself to do it.

Since he must have advisors, though, I'd like him to choose them because they're the best people he can find, not because they might fulfill a PR firm's idea of the best people he can find.

I deserve someone intelligent and inquisitive, who understands and appreciates people. I want a president who reads, who knows about history and other cultures, and respects those other cultures.

I want someone in the White House who can see that there might be more than two sides to a conflict, who can also see that in that same conflict it's not always true that one side deserves our support and the others don't—because all parties may be wrong.

I know my president must be a politician. He has to know how to deal with politicians, so he has to be one himself. But I want him to be interested in dealing with me, too. I want a president who believes that I have a right to know what's going on, and who will inform me in frank language, even if it's something I don't want to hear. If it's none of my business, I can appreciate that, but I want to know why it's none of my business.

I want a president who doesn't believe he's John Wayne, Don Juan, Andrew Carnegie, the Pope or Augustus Caesar.

Someone with a sense of humor would be nice. And I'd be thrilled if he consistently let us see how smart he is. Like, smarter than the rest of us. Imagine.

I guess I could just stop expecting anything of my president. But I'm not quite ready to do that. Besides, it doesn't seem right. If I give up, aren't I giving the president carte blanche to be stupid? If someone expects nothing of me, I'm likely to live up to that expectation.

These are reasonable demands. I have the right to expect intelligence, humility and curiosity of my president.

But if all that's too much to ask, then forget it and we'll make it just this. The Jews have a term for the kind of man I want to govern me: a "mensch"—a human being, a person.

I hope Obama is that kind of man. I'd appreciate it if he'd prove it to me. And keep proving it. Hail to the chief.

Jan. 8, 2009

FYI: But it first materialized on Jan. 13, 1989.

Why Not Ask Questions?

I DON'T WORK downtown anymore, haven't for over a year. So I don't spend as much time hanging around as I used to. So I imagine I'm the last person to have seen that addition to Central Square under the flag—the Pledge of Allegiance etched into the sidewalk.

I finally noticed it a couple of weeks ago. Instantly, I knew I'd write about it. It made me uneasy, for one thing. *Wow,* I thought. *Uneasy, in the middle of Auburn.* I told myself to be careful. Whatever I said about the fact of the Pledge on the sidewalk, I knew I'd make somebody mad.

You know me. You've read me for years. You know that Don and I stand at parades when the color guard marches past. Actually, we look forward to standing. We fidget. We race each other to see who leaps up first.

Plus we look for reasons to fly the flag at home. Flag Day! Election Day! Memorial Day, Veteran's Day, the Fourth of July! Not to mention our anniversary. And Thanksgiving.

So I think the flag's wonderful. The Pledge of Allegiance is just fine, too. I just get… itchy. Seeing it in Central Square feels like a demand that I subscribe to a specific, limited idea of patriotism.

I'm convinced the City Council members who voted 5-0 in favor of etching the Pledge on the sidewalk didn't expect me to feel this way. I know, too, that the outcome of the vote was a slam-dunk. Nobody in his right mind in politics in Auburn would dare to vote against this motion. The Pledge resides comfortably in that bag of unquestionable stuff that we call "traditional values."

But see, I have a terrible time with unquestionable stuff. I have this irresistible urge to ask questions.

No, no, relax. I don't want to get rid of the Pledge. I'm not necessarily complaining that it's there. I'm just—you know—asking questions.

And it's just that I'd appreciate seeing other, possibly patriotic references nearby. Why do they have just one patriotic statement on the sidewalk? Why not others?

Like, say, the Bill of Rights. Well, no, that would use up too much space, take up the whole sidewalk from Tre Pazzi to Hilda's.

So what about just my favorite, the First Amendment? "Congress shall make no law respecting an establishment of religion, or prohibiting the free exercise thereof; or abridging the freedom of speech, or of the press; or the right of the people peaceably to assemble, and to petition the Government for a redress of grievances." Be still, my heart.

Or the Preamble to the Constitution? "We the people of the United States, in order to form a more perfect union, establish justice, insure domestic tranquility, provide for the common defense, promote the general welfare, and secure the blessings of liberty to ourselves and our posterity, do ordain and establish this Constitution for the United States of America."

I wouldn't mind seeing this excerpt from the Declaration of Independence: "We hold these truths to be self-evident, that all men are created equal, that they are endowed by their Creator with certain unalienable Rights, that among these are Life, Liberty and the pursuit of Happiness."

Still too long? Well then, the heck with it. Let's just take Dr. Fox's "Why?" statue from the entrance to the Domes and move it downtown. Questioning our leaders, asking "Why?"—that's just about as patriotic as you can get. Certainly as patriotic as pledging allegiance to the flag.

###

June 24, 2012

ten

Auburn

WITH A CURRENT *population of 12,800, Auburn sits in California's Gold Country in the foothills of the Sierra Nevada, smack where Interstate 80 crosses Highway 49. It's the Placer County seat.*

I've always thought that the map of Placer County looks like a lopsided bow tie. Imagine that the west side of the tie sprawls into the Sacramento Valley, and the east side climbs to Lake Tahoe and Nevada. The knot of the bow? That's Auburn.

Like every town in every county in every state, Auburn has a history. Gold and the railroad, pears and apples, the American River and the Native Americans make up Auburn's.

Auburn's a wonderful place. It has its problems, like every town, but it also has dedicated people who care about what goes on and about its future.

This section gives you a taste of what it's like to live here. Don't be surprised if it sounds like life in your small town.

No Train I Wouldn't Take

I N THE FIELD behind my house, the westbound and eastbound Southern Pacific tracks come about as close to each
other as they ever do in Auburn. Trains pass so regularly and
I'm so accustomed to hearing them that I couldn't tell you how
many go by in a day.

But I always hear them coming. Each time my awareness shifts
from what I'm doing to the diesel engines rumbling outside my
window and the wheels hitting the seam in the westbound track
with an easy, comfortable rhythm.

The railroad carved out a deep ravine for the eastbound tracks,
so I can't see those trains when they pass. At night, though, I watch
for the engines' wavering lights reflected off the trees. During the
day if I look carefully I can follow the diesels' exhaust as they lum-
ber past.

The eastbound trains make more noise, too, since they're dragging their load uphill, through the foothills into the Sierra. Their
chugging echoes against the narrow walls, filling the neighborhood
in such a way that it's difficult to tell which direction they're coming
from.

Best of all, my landlord knows several of the engineers, and has
asked them to honk their horns as they go by his house—no matter
when they pass. Of course, the blasts have awakened me at three in

the morning. But that's okay. It's just fine to be awakened by a train.

When we tell people we live near the tracks, they tell us *oh, don't worry, you'll get used to it. Soon you won't hear the trains at all anymore.*

Don and I have decided we don't want to get used to them. To make sure of it, to ensure that we always pay attention, we announce the trains to each other. Both of us scheme to be first to announce a train to the other.

"Susan, a train," he says at dinner, raising his voice so that I can hear him over the rumbling. Or I'll go out to where he's raking leaves to inform him that a train's going by. But I have to be careful—if he hears me coming he'll beat me to it.

What is it about trains? By all rights, shouldn't they be obsolete? Aren't they an anachronism, especially in these last decades of the 20th century where freeways and airplanes are foremost in people's consciousness when they think of freight and transportation?

I'm intrigued by trains for several reasons—but I can find similar qualities in other vehicles. Yet those other, modern things leave me cold. Yes, trains are big and loud, but so are jets, buses, long-haul trucks and steamships. They travel coast to coast, but so do jets, buses, long-haul trucks and steamships.

Is it the variety? Consider the perfect names of the railroads: Atchison, Topeka and Santa Fe. Crab Orchard and Egyptian (I love that). Leavenworth, Pawnee and Western. Rock Island Line. Denver and Rio Grande. Marinette Tomahawk and Western. I've always liked Baltimore and Ohio. Closer to home: the long-defunct Nevada County Narrow-Gauge Railroad, also known fondly hereabouts as the Never Come Never Go.

Consider, too, the lovely and alliterative names of the locomotives. The Jupiter. City of San Francisco. Zephyr. Coastal Light. Sunset Limited. The Flying Scotsman. Old Ironsides. North Coast Limited.

I ask you: What other method of transportation common in the 1850s is still around in such numbers? Is there another method of transportation that has such a wildcat history? Can you think of another that gobbled up land so unprecedentedly, that found a way to navigate mountains and rivers once considered impassable?

Plus, the train's romantic. Don't ask me why. But let the CEO of Delta Airlines try to get away with that claim.

The nearly constant presence of trains is one of the reasons I'm pleased to live in Auburn. As I race out the door to wave at this latest engineer, I happily recall poet Edna St. Vincent Millay's wonderful line: "There isn't a train I wouldn't take, no matter where it's going."

Aug. 5, 1988

Stranger in My Neighborhood

I EYED THE stooped man as he wandered past my house. When Sam barked at him, he wavered uncertainly, staring at the windows. I stared back, hoping he couldn't see me as I made sure the screen door was latched. How weird he looked, with that phony black moustache and those thick black eyebrows.

On this warm morning, he wore a stocking cap and a heavy jacket. An old skillet hung from his disheveled bedroll. He'd stuffed one leg into a black, knee-high rubber boot. On his other foot, though, he wore a running shoe.

A crazy man, clearly. I continued to stare as he craned his neck at my house, then peered first one way up the empty street, then the other.

He looks lost. Clearly he needs help. But he's behaving in such a bizarre manner. Do I offer to help him? What if he's armed? What if he wants a place to sleep? What if he wants something I can't give? What if he really is crazy— what then?

Should I call the police? No—what would I tell them? A stranger's in the neighborhood? It's no crime to be a stranger, is it? No crime to be badly dressed, no crime to look like you need help or to look out of place—is it?

Finally he shuffled off, the skillet bouncing against his bedroll. Relieved, I figured that eventually he'd find the way back to the main road.

But here he comes again! Yow! Behaving exactly the same! Whoa—
Twilight Zone! Prickly neck time. I read the papers. I watch the news. It's no
crime to look out of place, mister, but look out of place in somebody else's neigh-
borhood.

A few minutes after he passed the house that second time, a
sheriff's patrol cruised by. I never saw him again.

Except—I see him all the time. Turns out this was my neighbor
Ernie, conducting an experiment.

A teenager during the Depression, he had watched as his mother
played hostess to the hobos passing through the Midwest by rail.

"She never turned a one of them down," he recalled. "She gave
them all a sandwich and an onion." Now, 65 years later, he wondered—would people treat him the way his mother treated those
nameless strangers? "I wanted to see how people would react if they
thought I was a bum," he told me.

Well, he found out. "Two people offered to help me," he said.
"Twelve people called the cops."

That deputy did approach him, he said. When she learned the
story—"I was just having a little fun, not doing any harm"—she
got a kick out of it.

"She put it in her log as a 'community joke,'" Ernie said. "And
she told me that the best thing that came out of it was that we
probably have the best neighborhood watch in town."

That may have been the best thing, but a number of other unnerving things came out as well. It says a great deal about society—
heck, about me—when a strangely dressed man who looks like he
needs help doesn't get it. He didn't conform to what I thought a
reasonable person should look like, so I dismissed him.

While I didn't call the police, I'm glad others did.

I'm sure Ernie expected the response he got. He's no dope. He recognizes the difference between the days of Hoover and these days, days of armed crack addicts, gangs and the mentally ill on the street.

It's not good, not a healthy time, and my reaction to that odd man outside is a reflection of this time. The malaise is in me, part of me. I'm not happy about it.

Ernie's lucky he lives in this neighborhood, this town. Some-place else? Somebody might have shot him.

Sept. 16, 1993

What a Community

K YNDRA BALDWIN IS 20 years old, starting her third year at Sierra College. A couple of weeks ago she was driving her '87 VW Golf down to her boyfriend's house in Newcastle, delivering $1,400 in cash so he could head to Los Angeles the next day and buy a speedway motorcycle.

"I was holding the money for him so he wouldn't spend it too soon," she said.

She had almost reached the Lincoln exit on I-80 when some odd stuff happened. Tailgated by some guy in a pickup, she moved into the slow lane to let him by. He was also being tailgated. As the second driver pulled up alongside her, the driver in front tapped his brake lights. The driver next to Kyndra swerved to the left, hit the center divider and caromed back. Kyndra, startled by the brake lights, swerved, tried to correct herself—and the second driver slammed into her.

Time slowed. Chaos took a while to happen. She watched as her Golf flew up, flipped twice and landed upside down on the shoulder. The windows blew out. Money flew everywhere. Fourteen hundred dollars scattered all over the car, outside, inside, under her head.

Lying there upside down, with a bloody nose, a scraped knee and a bruised chest from the seat belt, she stared out at the legs and feet that had suddenly materialized. People were everywhere, instantly.

"It was amazing, the amount of people who stopped," she said, and listed them: an off-duty policeman, physicians, people she'd never seen and won't see again. All of them were concerned, helpful, encouraging.

She was most grateful to nurse Michelle Warner, who works at the UC Davis Medical Group in Auburn. Michelle had seen the accident in her rearview mirror and "came back and sat with me and helped me find my money," Kyndra said. "She counted it several times. We got all of it but $105."

When the ambulance took Kyndra to Auburn Faith's emergency room, Michelle followed, bringing everything she could find out of the smashed Golf: photographs, car keys, notebooks, Kyndra's bowling ball. "She sat with me in the hospital, too," Kyndra said, "and called my mom and boyfriend."

"She didn't have anybody there," Michelle said. "I had an accident a couple years ago on Watt Avenue and nobody helped me. Nobody would phone for me. I know what it's like, and I didn't want it to happen to her.

"I know she felt funny, having a stranger hold all that money, but somebody had to gather it up. We found most of it."

Then, as the doctors stitched up her knee, a Highway Patrolman came in with the remaining $105. She got all the money back.

And when the tow truck returned her car, "I looked for my phone that nobody could find. It was right there, where it was supposed to be. It was wonderful. I'd heard about people taking things out of junked cars."

Indeed, she's heard the same stories you have about people who rob others when they're helpless and confused and hurt.

We've all heard about people in trouble in full view of others and nobody stops to help.

Kyndra's dad plays softball with Don, who came home after a game and shared this story with me. The more I heard, the more agitated I got, especially when I heard about all that money and all those people hanging around. I gritted my teeth and prepared to be disgusted. *Of course she wouldn't get her money back. Of course people's greed would surface. That's always the way, always, always...*

But the story kept getting better. People stopped—even physicians, in spite of these litigious times. Michelle stopped, ran back, stayed, helped, collected, followed and made phone calls. The cop didn't pocket the hundred bucks. And he could have, easily.

The more I heard, the prouder, the more impressed and amazed I felt. What a community.

"It was amazing how people pulled together to help," Kyndra said. "I feel really lucky, and really grateful. It was the scariest experience, that accident, but they made it so much better. They had no idea who I was."

"It felt really good to help her," said Michelle, who shrugs off the idea that she did anything extraordinary.

"I'd do it again."

What a great story.

Aug. 10, 1995

From the 2149 Guidebook

A UBURN: POPULATION 623,011. Elevation: 1,253.
Welcome to this charming, bustling village in the Gold
Country foothills. We hope you will enjoy this self-guided
tour of the many interesting sites illustrating the stimulating history
of this Placer County jewel.

Stop 7: At the intersection of Luther Boulevard and the dou-
ble-decker section of Highway 49 is the site of the last locally-
owned business in Auburn. The restoration of this now-defunct,
enchanting but obsolete way of doing business represents the typical small size of the building as well as the inadequate 60-foot sign
advertising the presence of this company.

Stop 19: You've reached one of the prime tourist spots of
Auburn, here at the Overlook of the George Beland Multi-Purpose
Dam. For years the dam has lured hundreds of thousands of boat-
ers, water skiers and swimmers to the pristine natural beauty of Beland Lake.

Off to your right is one of the busiest spots, the Information
Booth, where you can see old holographs of what this view once
looked like before the dam was built: the confluence of the North
and Middle forks of the Doolittle (once American) River, the
crumbling No Hands Bridge, Diver's Bar and Mammoth Bar. Here
you can also see samples of the wildlife—cute but economically

worthless—that used to live here. These irrelevant species benefited considerably as a result of the protection plan that relocated them when the dam was built.

Stop 37: This, the first warehouse store in Auburn, is built on what once was called "Old Town Auburn." This warehouse is typical of the times. Note the space-wasting flowerbeds and the pointless architecture that tried to disguise the boxy shape. Note, too, all the benches placed in a futile effort to accommodate people's tired feet. We have since realized that nothing short of golf carts can solve the problem of tired feet when shopping in warehouses.

Stop 41a: Years ago, Maple Street was the first entrance to Auburn off the I-80 Interstate going east. Highway historians, working with archaeologists, also tell us that at this spot the interstate was comprised of only three lanes in each direction.

Stop 41b: Here in front of you is what's left of what many experts claim was the bed of Auburn Ravine, where Claude Chana discovered gold in Auburn. Except for this puddle, the stream is no longer visible. Instead, it is now rerouted and cemented over to make room for the enclosed 837-store Ralph Swann Memorial Mall.

Stop 59: This softball field is preserved as an example of the kind of recreational extravagance practiced by Auburn natives at the end of the 20th century. Once, four or five (!) of these fields took up several acres of prime real estate, a problem that soon needed solving. The answer came in the Auburn High Rise Recreational Facility and Garage, located—as you can see—along the left field line of the old-fashioned diamond. Within this circular 17-story building that appears to be solely for parking are three soccer, five softball and four football fields, all carpeted with Astroturf.

Stop 93: This, the Sanborn-Couzens Corner, contains samples of "books," those inefficient, space-eating monsters that people once used to find information before the invention of the CD-ROM. These "books" were stored in a building called a "library."

Stop 107: On this site was Auburn's first skyscraper, a modest 43-story charmer. It boasted such tenants as the village's seven radio stations, the Tahoe Club and the offices of the Auburn Rams before they went back to Los Angeles.

Stop 111: Here you see a "tree," growing in a "vacant lot," surrounded by various "native plants" called "weeds." This site, long called the Eric Peach Zone, has been hotly debated for years, ever since it was discovered that this is the last piece of undeveloped land within city limits. The mysterious Peach, however, stipulated in his will that this property could not be touched for 200 years after his death, and no amount of legal maneuvering has been able to lift this edict.

Feb. 22, 1996

Small-Town Excitement

FOUR OR FIVE YEARS AGO, when I was still in charge of publicity for the Auburn Area Christmas Basket Program, Don and I drove our pickup in the Festival of Lights Parade. With a Christmas Basket banner on both sides, we promoted the program, honking the horn and waving at everybody. Such goings on, such crowds, such festivity! That parade is one of those events where your face gets tired from grinning all the time.

We set up afterwards in the National Guard Armory, getting set for the crowd to join us for Santa, kids' games, hot dogs, cotton candy, etc. etc. As other early birds straggled in—long before the parade had ended—a scruffy guy approached me and asked where he could get something to eat.

I looked at him and wondered—*a transient? On the way to Reno? Who knows?*—as I considered his question. I told him he could wait a little and see if somebody set up something in the Armory.

Or—I considered some more. It wasn't the middle of the afternoon, when tons of places are open for lunch. Plus I'm not good at giving directions quickly.

I tried, but I fizzled.

He finally glared at me. "This is a really nothing town," he sneered. "There's nothing going on here."

I barked with laughter as he stalked off, studiously ignoring the hubbub surrounding him, oblivious to the fuss and commotion and celebration a block away.

I thought of him the Sunday after the Black & White Ball. On one of my several errands that day, I met a guy, probably in his mid-20s, who jovially asked, "Well, anything exciting going on out there?"

I never know how to answer questions like that. I think of too much and too little to say, and I dry up. *Depends*, I think. *Define your terms*. I imagine he asked me only to be saying something. Probably he was convinced that I didn't know anything about what's really exciting. Especially when he complained about how boring Auburn is.

Huh? Auburn? Boring? Really? Gee—how come I'm not bored, then? What did he have in mind, Las Vegas? Drive-by shootings? Fistfights on every corner? Rap music in the street?

He said he'd just moved here. Why, I asked, since he found the town so boring. He doesn't have to live here.

To be closer to his daughter and her mother, he said. Ah, well. He'd found some excitement once, anyway.

To be honest, I did have an answer for this guy. I told him I'd gotten the news that the library would present Silver Screen Classic Movies again next year. That was exciting, I said. And I'd already set the movie schedule, ordered the movies, chosen the publicity photos. All that's exciting.

I could have gone on, and would have, but I watched him waiting for me to finish. My examples bore no resemblance to his idea of excitement. He probably wanted a rock concert every weekend.

My mother had a wonderful old saw that she pulled out at the least encouragement. "None is so blind as he who will not see," she'd intone to her children when we couldn't find a toothbrush or the solution to a long-division problem.

Those two guys who thought Auburn such a nothing town—they'd have stared blankly back at her, shrugged, and walked away. They don't have the eyes to see, caught as they are in their narrow definitions.

I mean, the first guy passed judgment during the Festival of Lights Parade. The second sniffed at the town's "nothingness" the day after the Black & White Ball, an event that yearly prompts irate letters to the editor complaining about the noise and crowds. Boring? A town that promotes and hosts an event that loud?

I guess that wasn't what he had in mind, though. All right—had he been to the river lately? Had he attended a fractious City Council meeting, or participated in the Auburn Skate Park debate? Has he sat in on one of the latest rounds of the Airport Commission fight? Has he even heard of the Auburn Art Walk? Does he attend the Auburn Symphony performances? What about Fast Fridays at the Gold Country Fairgrounds?

Of course, it's not my job to point out to others the exciting aspects of my small town. It's my job to find them on my own. If others can't see what I see, that's not my fault.

Sept. 28, 2000

No Town Is Unique

I DIDN'T ALWAYS buy newspapers when I traveled. Years ago, driving from state to state, I'd mope because the papers I saw weren't familiar, didn't talk about stuff and places I knew. They weren't the ones I was used to. So what was the point of picking up these odd, out-of-town strangers? Talk about being stuck.

Since I've been connected with the *Journal,* however, wherever I go I seek out the local papers. Once, I paid no attention to the public private lives of the people who lived in the towns I drove through. Now I can't get enough of them.

I love them. Because these papers all resemble one another. By this, I mean that all the stories are the same. Every town has its scandals, the local boy who's made good and its city council scrapping with each other each week. Each paper has its features section and a story and photo about last weekend's fundraising fete at the Elks Lodge, photos of children leaping in puddles, a thriving letters to the editor section.

We like to think Auburn is a one-of-a-kind kind of place, but it isn't. Consider Richard Yue, who does wonderful things for this community, and received the McCann Award as a result. Good for him. He deserves it.

Although Richard does great things for Auburn, a person doing great things for his town is not unique. People do great things for their towns everywhere—and that's wonderful.

When Don and I meandered around South Dakota, Colorado, Wyoming and Nebraska last fall, I did what I do best when I travel: I hunted for local newspapers.

I found a lovely jewel in a weekly I picked up in tiny Ogallala, Nebraska—on Interstate 80 on the Platte River. It was a letter of gratitude from a native, a man who had coached local football for over 30 years. The town had honored him by naming the new high school football stadium after him.

I loved everything about it: the town's motives, his reaction, his motives behind his long years of service, the kids he'd started with—kids who now have kids of their own. This was so familiar. You find good people everywhere, not just Auburn.

His gratitude was obvious. The sense of community was obvious (the way it is in Auburn). People had conspired to do something they knew would touch him. It worked, and he said so.

I'd never heard of this community, a town filled with people I'll never meet. Most likely you never will, either. But it was a big thing to a lot of people.

When I teach writing, I discuss secondary characters: they need to be as clear in the writer's mind as the main characters. Even a secondary character is a person. He doesn't think he's a secondary character. Like the woman in the grocery store stocking the milk, or the UPS deliveryman.

Sure, they're just on the periphery of your attention, but they have full lives, families, dreams. You just don't know about them. Just as they don't know about your dreams or your family, because you're only on the periphery of their attention. And heaven knows, you're not a secondary character.

The movers and shakers, big deal publishers of big deal magazines, big deal producers of big deal TV programs—they focus on other big deal movers and shakers in big deal cities on the coasts, implying that anyone doing anything anywhere else is just wasting time.

Hah.

In other news: On Saturday, Don and I visited my sister and brother-in-law in tiny Mountain Ranch, down Highway 49 in Calaveras County, about 10 miles from San Andreas. Bill had some lines in the homegrown musical, a fundraiser to renovate the town hall.

The show included dinner served by an enthusiastic, energetic crew of women that included my sister. The town hall, almost as big as the Gold Country Fairgrounds' Sierra Building, was packed with people delighted to be there, happy to see their neighbors and pleased to contribute to the renovation.

The last words on the program encouraged donations to the community club, "which is entrusted with keeping this treasured old building up to snuff for this treasured old community." Ahh. Sweet.

Everything about this event—the energy, the organization and the camaraderie—reminded me of Auburn. It reinforced my idea that, like newspapers, all close communities are the same.

March 7, 2002

Our Work in Progress

MAN, IT WAS hot. Of course, it was July. It was Auburn. Naturally it would be hot. In the process of moving here, I'd looked for apartments all day and I was hungry. I stumbled up the steps of the Pullen House and had one of the best salmon dinners I can remember. Oh, my.

Some of you wouldn't remember the Pullen House. At least, you wouldn't remember it as a place to eat. It's the porched house on Lincoln Way, now a salon across from Luigi's. Which wasn't always Luigi's, which is in the block up from the A.R.T.S. building, which used to be Foothills Furniture, which was several doors up from Leatherby's ice cream parlor.

My husband Don and I moved here in August of 1985. Eighteen years ago. My goodness. Babies born the year we came are settling on what college to go to next year.

I had coffee with a newcomer last week at Depoe Bay (you know, where Flowers by Footes used to be before it moved across the street). Last August, Mary moved here from San Jose to get married. She and her husband live in a South Auburn neighborhood east of Shirland Tract, off of Auburn-Folsom overlooking the canyon. In fact, I'll bet if she stands in the right place, she can see where the cofferdam used to be.

On that incredibly stormy day when the cofferdam broke, I was driving our old, tired, yellow Datsun 1200 and had just parked in the Alpine Grocery lot at Elm and 49 (where Staples is now, and where the Bank of Alex Brown was; across 49 from Safeway. Remember Safeway—now Pack 'n Save on Bell? And Thrifty?) And I heard Jim Huggins on KAHI break the news about the dam. I raced through the downpour, slopped into the grocery store and watched the gray sky empty itself.

So to my astonishment, Auburn started changing the moment I moved here. When I arrived, I expected things to stay the way I'd found them. Actually they were in the middle of changing. It just took me a while to realize it.

So Mary lives here now, and things are the way they are. Auburn probably feels pretty static to her, and if she's anything like I was, she might expect things to stay this way. The name of the hospital is Sutter Auburn Faith, instead of Auburn Faith Community. The parking lot at the corner of Bell and 49 serves Target, rather than the North Fork Dry Diggins restaurant. The Auburn Village shopping center inhabits the territory north of the intersection of New Airport Road and 49, instead of a field with Yamasaki's Nursery in the middle of it.

If she goes into the *Auburn Journal* to drop off a press release for any reason, she'll probably consider the brick-floored lobby and the high ceiling basic and ordinary. This is what the *Journal* office looks like, why make a fuss about it? But geez, if you want basic and ordinary, I offer the newspaper office the way it used to be, for heaven's sake. I mean, in 1986, when I first got involved with the paper, the place was a mess, cramped and crazy and dark.

As a relative newcomer, there's so much Mary doesn't know. She doesn't know who Ralph Swann was, for example, and I didn't have all the words necessary to explain him to her. He'd have done a much better job, and gone on longer, but he's not around anymore.

She arrived too late for last year's Music on the Green, the American River Confluence Festival and the Artie Awards. She doesn't know the history of the ACPC Art Walk or the Studio Tour or the We Love Our Library Dinner. She doesn't remember Auburn before the Auburn Arts Commission, Auburn Community Television, the Fall Harvest Festival or the Festival of Lights Parade. In her experience, the Auburn Symphony has always existed.

All of these are an integral part of this place, yet they all arrived after I did.

I tell everyone that Auburn is a work in progress. I didn't always think so. I was the only change I expected to see. When I arrived, I assumed Auburn would remain the same. But it did, I finally realized. It was in the middle of changing, and it's stayed that way. Change is a constant, no matter what I expect or have in mind. And even though I still feel like a newcomer, it's astonishing to think about all the changes I've seen since I came.

And in 18 years, Mary will say the same thing.

Feb. 20, 2003

Congratulating This Community

I SPENT HIGH school trying to be invisible. Straining to avoid attracting attention to myself, feeling frizzy-haired, ungainly, inadequate and freckled, I tiptoed through those years as silently as possible.

Reading "Rikki Tikki Tavi," about Kipling's heroic mongoose in India, I identified most closely with Chuchundra the muskrat, not Rikki or the cobras. Chuchundra could never muster the nerve to leave the safety of the wall and run into the middle of the room.

Well, you're reading evidence that I've changed. I'm proud to say that I can finally run out in the middle of the room.

Recently, I attended Placer High's Senior Awards Ceremony, an event that celebrated 18-year-olds whose high school years look nothing like mine. These young people have felt comfortable in attracting attention to themselves, exposing their smarts and energy, running out into the middle of the room far sooner than I did.

As president of the Auburn Branch of the American Association of University Women, I was there to present the Leona Bivens Memorial Scholarship award.

It was a thrill, for a lot of reasons. For one thing, I wasn't alone. In the presenters' section, I sat holding a program that listed six pages of awards—awards and scholarships given by service groups, community groups, individuals, universities and the high school.

These awards recognized hard work, concerted effort, high grades and determination.

"It was fabulous," said JoAnn Wojcik, president of the Kiwanis Club of Auburn, who presented four awards that night. "We love giving out money. Our motto is 'serving the children of the world one community at a time.' I was really proud to represent Kiwanis, and those awards were well deserved."

"There was great joy in the room," said Ruth Johanson, who awarded the third Theodore L. Johanson Memorial Scholarship, to honor not only a student's quality work but also her late husband, through the Placer Cal Alumni Association.

She loves these ceremonies. "There were all the proud family members, and I was touched by the closeness of the class—there was such congeniality among them."

"They're a nice group," said Kathy Connelly, 2005-2006 PHS Senior Counselor, who received enthusiastic huzzahs from the green-robed group in the center of the auditorium whenever she appeared. And she appeared often: She handed out 33 awards, from the high school and from organizations that ranged from Soroptimists and the Italian Catholic Federation to the Auburn Optimists and the Elks. This doesn't include the scholarships from UC Davis, UCSB, UCSC and others.

Bob Bunge, who presented three awards, has participated in these ceremonies since 1982. "It's important to recognize them," he said. "And it's rewarding for them to see that the community acknowledges their hard work. That's really important for teenagers."

All these organizations, all these individuals recognizing these energetic and happy students. Sitting there, thrumming with excitement, I felt gratified by so much participation. And the kids—they got such pleasure out of each other's success. Their cheers for their comrades were wholehearted and incessant.

This helps make a community: public and enthusiastic support and encouragement of its young people.

I came away with something even more important that night. We like to think we're unique, but if we behave or think a certain way, others do, too.

So if Placer High held an awards ceremony on May 22, with community members and service groups recognizing the hard work of its students, this was happening in other towns in Placer County. Not only in Placer, either—in other towns in other counties all over the state, and in other states all over the country.

It happens here, so it happens other places. Imagine: thousands of high school seniors applauding one another. Imagine: thousands of service groups and community organizations publicly recognizing the success of those students. Imagine: millions of dollars awarded for scholarship, thinking, effort, wisdom and achievement.

Even better: This is an annual event. It happened last year, the year before that, ten years ago, 37, 71, a hundred years ago. It'll happen again next year.

This wonderful armor gives me such hope. I felt so warmed, so lifted, so impressed. I congratulate us all: students, school and community.

May 25, 2008

A Valentine to My Small Town

WELL! TOMORROW'S VALENTINE'S Day. Periodically, Don's friends ask him what he'll get me, and he always tells them the same thing: nothing. Huh? Nothing? Right, he says, explaining that I don't approve of Valentine's Day. *She's just saying that,* they insist. *She really wants you to get her something. Better do it, or you'll be in trouble.* No, Don says. She means it.

Right. I mean it. I think it's just a ploy to push people to spend money, and to promote the unpalatable idea of saving this one day to express your love. I don't like advertising executives telling me what to do.

Even so, now seems as good a time as any to tell you that I have enough of what I need for Valentine's Day. My cup runneth over with affection for and from this town. We have the wonderful We Love Our Library Dinner, the wonderful Symphony, fabulous merchants—to begin with. Who could ask for anything more?

I have an example of what I mean. What I want to tell you is not news. News is current; this is not.

Last December, I attended a Board of Supervisors' meeting. I don't regularly go to these things, even though I know I should. However, this time I went because the Board honored Mark Parker, the retiring Director of Library Services. I had a wonderful time, not only because I was surrounded by Mark Parker fans.

No—Mark was only one of many people the Supervisors honored that day. Others, like D.A. Brad Fenocchio and Public Information Officer Anita Yoder, were also retiring.

But the rest of them? Their only connection with the County was that they live here. According to that day's agenda, the Board honored them because of "their acts of heroism, longstanding community service or exceptional acts that have dramatically improved or impacted people's lives."

Lots of applause and standing ovations. Lots of admiration and respect and expressions of gratitude.

These awards went to people who had no expectation of receiving an award. Serving the community was their intention—serving because they loved what they were doing and the people they served, and their love was their only expected compensation.

I remembered attending an awards ceremony to honor exceptional graduating seniors at Placer High. I realized that, because we're not unique, if this high school honored exceptional seniors, other high schools in other towns all over the state also honored exceptional seniors. Not to mention high schools in other towns in other states. And this wasn't a one-time event. This had happened last year, and 30 years ago, and it would happen next year and the year after that.

So it must be with these awards from the Supervisors to these citizens, I thought. If it happens here, it happens elsewhere. It gave me wonder great as my content to imagine other exceptional private citizens in previous years also receiving well-deserved recognition from the Board of Supervisors—as well as private citizens of other counties in California being similarly honored.

And if this happens in California, it also happens in other states.

Wonderful people in this wonderful county do wonderful things. And because we are not unique, we must recognize that people in other counties also perform acts of heroism and lovingly serve their communities and change people's lives in stunning and impressive ways.

Love comes in many forms. It's thrilling to think about, the day before Valentine's Day.

Feb. 13, 2011

FYI: I know, I repeat the message from the previous column. But what a nice, uplifting, positive message to repeat. And what a pleasure to repeat it.

The Music Makes Me Better

MICHAEL GOODWIN WOULD not be pleased. The maestro and artistic director of the Auburn Symphony has told me more than once that listening to music means just that: listening to music. *Pay attention,* he says. *Listen to what it's doing,* he says, *and where it's going. Hear it.*

Of course he's right. When I sit in the audience with the Symphony's gorgeous—and gorgeously-performed—music sweeping over me, I know I will do myself a favor if I will just let myself listen.

But I'm so gratified at what I'm hearing, and what they're doing for me and with me and to me, always so impressed, that in addition to listening I start thinking about other things. Like the communication going on between the musicians and Michael, between them and me, between them and the music, between them and the composers.

Or I think about the brilliant composers of this incredible music. They're usually dead, but their work still moves me to tears. How my reaction would satisfy them, I think. Even a century—or centuries—later.

And I consider the elegant and eloquent teamwork occurring in front of me. These people didn't coincidentally arrive here at this moment with the nifty idea to just suddenly make music together. This collaboration involved thought and care and talent and time.

And I think about the gift these people give to me and them-selves and the community. What a vital contribution to a civilized society: people coming together to make beautiful music, to uplift themselves and others, to make themselves and others happy. It's such a wonderful thing I have tears even as I type these words. Oh, it's magnificent.

Do you understand how these thoughts could distract me from the music? Well, you see my difficulty. The more I'm impressed, the less I think about letting myself listen. Because I'm so impressed. What a wonderful problem.

In other news, sort of: I received a heated email from a reader in response to my column two weeks ago. "Outrage takes up a lot of energy," I wrote, "sapping me of the humor necessary to live energetically and kindly and carefully. It's hard to love my fellow man while gnashing my teeth. It's hard to stoke my fury and con-tribute to my community at the same time."

"You must not be trying very hard," snapped this reader. "Fighting evil and corruption and injustice (isn't) contributing to the community? ...As Eleanor Roosevelt put it, 'The only life worth living is a fighting life.' Dare anyone say she did not 'contrib-ute to the community'?

"Enjoy the view from your easy chair as you read a good book and sip your tea. I will be in the arena."

My tossed-off response: "Living a kind life, contributing and sharing and giving blood and voting and loving: This is fighting evil and corruption and injustice."

Last Sunday, sitting in the Placer High Auditorium balcony, en-thralled by the Symphony, I thought of a less-than-tossed-off response. Yeah, even as I should have been paying attention to the music.

If, as this reader believes, the only life worth living is a fighting life, that puts the Symphony in the middle of the fight, smack inside that arena. Their art fills and enlightens us. It makes us all larger and better. These musicians push away darkness and open spaces for the light. What better way to fight ugliness?

And what about those of us who jump to our feet in response to their talent? We're part of the fight, too. Watch us as we make our civilization more civilized.

April 24, 2011

FYI: Michael Goodwin died in a car accident the February following publication of this column. His loss was/is deeply felt, but the Symphony goes on, continues to thrive. The Symphony has hired a new conductor/artistic director, Peter Jaffe, and I get to continue sharing my time, my life and my joy in this wonderful music with others who feel the same way. The music makes us better. For information, check out the website: auburnsymphony.com

eleven

Tschitska

HUH? YEAH, WELL, I don't blame you. You wouldn't be the first to do a double take at this or another word from the Rushtonian vocabulary. We have several. Many are unprintable. As a result we have to shake ourselves before we leave the house, so we remember to speak the right language.

Don and I made up tschitska years ago. It's a dish with everything in it, if by everything you mean onions and peppers and garlic. Meat of some sort is usually involved. If you have some mushrooms, they go in; if you don't, they don't. If you have some cheap wine, it goes in there; plus good tomatoes, if this is summer. If you have a can of corn, sure, throw that in, too. Don wouldn't argue if you boiled up some vermicelli.

In other words, the Rushton version of stone soup. Or mulligan stew. Whatever you have hanging around.

So this section includes pieces that might not have anything to do with each other. If you see a connection, great. If you don't, I wouldn't be surprised.

Just a Pretty Face

CONSIDER TWO CARS, please. The first: a new BMW 535, with 182 horsepower and 209 cubic inch engine, electric dual position sunroof, heated outside mirrors, electrically adjustable leather seats and 523 miles on car and radial tires.

The second car? Oh, say it's a Chevrolet, a 23-year-old Caprice with automatic transmission, the broken odometer registering 231,053 miles (103,071 of these on the second engine), a back window stuck open, a surly swipe of primer on the otherwise black hood, and a bashed in right fender, otherwise blue.

Or that second car could be an irritable Toyota Corona, demanding a quart of oil every month and shuddering at idle like the paint shaker in a hardware store. Or it could be a (mostly) beige 1971 Volkswagen beetle, saddled with ragged seat covers and a ragged hole in the muffler.

Now tell me: Which car would you rather own? Which would you feel most comfortable driving? Which would you trust round trip to St. Louis, and which would give you years of freedom from mechanical headaches?

Which car would send the DMV and loan officers and insurance agents into paroxysms of avarice?

Or say your teenager begs to borrow the car to shlep his buddies to the movies (opening night of Halloween XVIII) or to the football game (traditional rivals, rabid fans) or to the mountains (first big ski weekend). Which keys do you absently toss him—afterwards really concentrating on Michael Jordan?

Yes, I've recently bought a new car, a modest Honda Accord. As I made the rounds of the dealers, I finally saw the open sore I'd been driving around: the Zero, my Datsun 1200, still gasping after 17 years and 240,000 miles, its madly multiplying rust stains resembling freckles on a Little Leaguer.

The Zero embarrassed me, especially after I brought the Honda home. At last I owned a car with a heater that didn't double as an open window; a car with decent brakes and no sullen leak in the differential; a new car whose compression levels didn't resemble Dolly Parton's measurements.

Yet, because it was new, I encountered problems I'd never expected. Suddenly the most benign situations unnerved me. Parking in a narrow space in a crowded lot seemed the most foolhardy behavior. Once a tempting invitation to potential adventure, an untested road twisting into the hills now threatened rather than beckoned. Visions of branches, rocks, potholes, or all three—or all three at night—loomed before me.

Yet the threat of splotches or scrapes had never given me a moment's pause in the Zero. One more dent wouldn't make any difference. Not on an old car.

Sure, the Honda may be many things, but it is not old. And because of this, I suddenly yearn for the only things this new car lacks: character and history. The Datsun, now. I certainly wouldn't trust it on that trip to St. Louis, but I remember when I could—and did. I remember when, during a January sunrise in Death Valley, the odometer pushed past 100,000 miles. I know the story behind that gash in the rear bumper (I backed into a boulder in Idaho).

There are other Datsun 1200s, but none like this one. It's impossible to lose in a crowded parking lot. Not like the Honda, or that BMW with the nifty dual position sunroof. I see others exactly like them, lots of them, all smooth and unmarked, like one of those lean teenagers you see at the beach or at Burger King. Sure, they're attractive enough, but with their perfect teeth and uncreased skin, they all look alike. They have no identity, no individuality.

But check out that sagging, blue-gray Valiant across the street with the missing left headlight. Or, in front of the post office, that old MG with the roped-down trunk and torn cloth top. There's individuality for you. What's the story behind them?

Heck—newness isn't everything. It runs a distant second to character for keeping my attention.

Nov. 22, 1987

FYI: For you youngsters: Datsun morphed into Nissan in 1986.

No Shabby Prejudices, Thanks

A STRANGER APPROACHES my group at a party and tells us a story—he'd call it a joke—about a man with a harelip. We tolerate him. He finishes that story, and before he starts the next one, asks, "Any Catholics here?"

"I'm not Catholic," I say, "but my brother has a harelip." He doesn't, but the guy will never know I'm lying. It shuts him up, which is all I want.

Some years later, I worked in a real estate office. I'm sure one of my coworkers never saw me with my mouth closed because she kept saying things like "This couple says the house costs too much. But they're Jewish, you know, and th-o-o-se pe-e-ople have ways of getting more money."

At a party, she and I and another woman discussed an absent fourth: "She converted to Judaism," she said. "Nice person, though."

If she hadn't been the boss's daughter, I'd have told her—what? I don't know. Maybe "Rosemary, you're too intelligent to talk like that." Or "Shut up." Something. I knew I couldn't change her mind.

Instead, I loaned her my copy of Leo Rosten's *The Joys of Yiddish*, a book I love that has taught me a great deal. "I thought you might be interested," I said as I gave it to her.

"Thank you," she said graciously, because she could be very

gracious. But I could see her thinking, *Rushton… it doesn't sound Jewish, but tho-o-se pe-e-ople…*

As a result, she never expressed her prejudice to me again. I was satisfied. That's all I could have hoped for, anyway.

And that's all I really want. In the best of all possible worlds, everyone of every sex, color, religion and ethnic group accepts each other. I don't live in that world, so I want to live in the second best—in which there's bias but I don't know about it.

I have my prejudices, but it's a great source of pride to me that you don't know what they are. And I consider it no honor if you share yours with me. Just because I'm the same color as you, or the same sex, age or religion doesn't mean we think the same or live our lives the same. If you feel some sort of buddy-buddy emotion and wish to show me what a "regular guy" you are by showering me with "us vs. them" tales or slurs that were coined to offend to begin with, please restrain yourself.

I'm hollering like this because I recently had to be polite to a man at a gathering I attended. He was older than I, and I've been taught to be polite to my elders, as well as how to be a good guest. So, being a good guest, I listened as he spouted his racist phrases. I felt obligated to call him on it, though—so I kept asking him what he meant, as calmly as I could.

But the others' silence seemed to frown at me rather than at him, as if I were the ill-mannered one. My inability to quietly tolerate his intolerance embarrassed those around me. *Shh, Susan. Don't make a scene. That's just the way he talks. Don't mind him.*

But I do mind him. I mind his inflicting his shabby prejudices on me. What, it's OK for him to offend me, but not OK for me to make it clear that I'm offended and ask him to stop? Must I tolerate his offensiveness because "that's just the way he is"?

Well, what about me? What if "the way I am" involves swearing at formal gatherings or picking my nose, regardless of who's around me?

I don't believe people would tolerate that, would brush off that behavior, humor me with a mild chuckle. And they shouldn't. Sure, this is a "free country," but I'm convinced that I have an obligation to oblige others, to encourage civilized behavior in this civilization.

But don't make me the only one saddled with that responsibility. I'm tired of being polite to impolite people, tired of implicitly encouraging crude behavior by shutting up.

But don't mind me. That's just the way I am.

June 22, 1988

FYI: I was so mad when I wrote this column that I don't remember typing it. Just looked up and there it was on the screen. That doesn't happen very often.

Consider Raku

THE KILN ROARS. Inside, the pots glow red-yellow. Nearby wait bins of straw, buckets of water, and students—the artists responsible for the creations now baking in the oven.

Finally comes the time for outside action. Armed with special tongs, her hands thickly gloved, the first student grasps the closest red-hot bowl. She maneuvers it to the straw and sets it down. The straw ignites instantly.

A risk: The straw can't burn too long, but it must burn, and the artist can't make quick moves or she risks spreading the fire or breaking her handiwork. Both are possible.

After a moment, the student takes the tongs and grasps the flaming mass again. She steps to the bucket of water. She lowers it in. The water boils. It fumes and hisses, like the ocean surrounding a molten lava flow.

The moment the flames die, she removes the charred bowl, tendrils of black hay stuck to it, and sets it on a board to cool.

Later, she cleans off the blackened thing. What she uncovers may bear no resemblance to what she expects. The glaze that results in a specific color and texture when fired in the standard manner won't behave predictably when the piece is subjected to this violent treatment.

The color isn't predictable, nor is the integrity of the piece—it might not survive the trip from fire to water—nor is the pattern that appears as a result of the rapid heating and cooling. Fine lines resembling a road map of Ohio cover the shiny glaze. Each piece is unique, with its own pattern of lines, unlike any other subjected to the same treatment.

This is the process of Raku pottery. With Raku, the only thing the potter knows for sure is that she knows nothing is for sure.

If you come to the studio loaded with expectations, expect to be disappointed. If you come to the studio intending to dominate the situation, confident that there's something concrete you can do to control the outcome of the violent meeting of clay, glaze, fire and water—expect to be disappointed.

Come, instead, prepared to be surprised, ready to accept anything as long as it's whole and its form resembles what you started out with—lo, happiness.

I love Raku. I love the risk, the unpredictability and the futility of forming expectations. I love the need to be at peace, whatever the result.

I need Raku. At least I need its philosophy. Because I get so annoyed with myself sometimes, when words I've worked hard on don't turn out the way I wanted them to. As a result, I denigrate them, even though others might say they're wonderful. What do they know? I think. After all, the piece didn't conform to what I was sure I wanted. Some may find good things in these bastard children. And while I acknowledge all compliments, I shrug inside. The piece didn't come out the way I wanted, so how could it be any good?

I'm not alone, either. People have high expectations of themselves, their spouses, their children, meals they cook, jobs they perform, photographs they take. The list is endless.

Yet things often don't turn out the way we expect. And when we believe we know exactly what we're looking for, we're disappointed when we don't find it. We tend not to look beyond our original—and often very narrow—expectations.

Behaving otherwise requires a considerable and deliberate mental shake, a giant change of attitude. If I can put my expectations aside and accept the results of my efforts—as long as they're solid and whole—lo, happiness. And expanded horizons as well, when I allow myself to explore beyond my one narrow road of expectations.

I need to be ready to be surprised, and to accept that surprise. Life's an adventure. I need to embrace Raku.

###

Feb. 9, 1990

Connected in Washington

O
H, YES, THOUSANDS of tourists clog Washington, D.C. every day. And everybody has the same stories to tell: viewing the Lincoln Memorial in the moonlight, seeing not nearly enough of the Smithsonian and listening to some boring schlub of a senator orating to a nearly empty Senate chamber.

I have those stories myself, but I'll save them for another time. Two events from my recent trip eclipse my memories of aching feet and the marble steps leading to the vision of Lincoln's craggy face.

Approaching the east entrance (the back door) of the Capitol, we heard the fuss and fume of a protest group. Soon we saw about 100 people crowded onto the steps, waving banners, chanting and beating drums.

A demonstration, hot dog—and we looked for the ubiquitous network cameras and the mass of reporters.

Nothing doing. Just a bunch of people protesting at the Capitol, objecting to the policies of the current administration. I forget which policies, because I was so impressed that no one from the media was present.

So the media ignored them. Not only that, none of the crowds of people milling around—tourists, cops, formal types in dark suits and red power ties—paid any attention either. Just me.

I asked one of the cops how often people staged protests there.

Every day, he answered, shrugging. Sometimes more. So many, in fact, have the same goal that they have to make appointments downtown so they don't conflict.

Wow. Imagine living in a country with a government that guarantees me the right of free speech and assembly, even if I think its policies stink and want to tell it so. Imagine a country with a government so willing to accommodate my exercising my right to tell it where to get off that it arranges things so that I get my chance to say so. I get chills thinking about it.

Later, in the echoing, five-floor Longworth House Office Building—endless, the ceilings distant, the floors marble—we stand outside massive polished double doors, the entrance to, the dignified sign sedately informs us, the House Ways and Means Committee Hearing Room.

We try the knob. It's unlocked. Boldly, we enter. It's empty. It's quiet. Like the rest of Longworth, it's far from modest. Chandeliers hang from distant ceilings, sharing space with track lights clearly installed to accommodate television cameras. Windows start at the floor and rise to meet those ceilings.

Rows of chairs at one end of the room face tables with microphones ready for witnesses; these tables in turn face a vast dais that extends the width of the other end of the room, a dais with plenty of room for chairs, writing space and more microphones.

We, in jeans and running shoes, don't belong in this august place. We're too pedestrian for such a formal setting. We look at each other. *We should leave. We should leave now. Before someone finds us here.*

But I can't help it. I'm a nosy reporter. Reckless, heart in my mouth—*this is none of my business! Any minute the authorities will storm in and evict us!*—I step up on the dais and edge down the row of chairs.

I open a drawer. An acorn rattles around this otherwise empty cranny.

I love that acorn. I know how it got there. It caught the eye of some faceless committee member who thought it was interesting, enjoyed the colors, liked the feel of it against his fingers and brought it to work. Later that week, as a witness droned an answer to someone else's question, he rediscovered the acorn in his pocket and eased his official life a bit by indulging again in the pleasure of inspecting it.

Yes, we breathed in some Smithsonian treasures. We viewed the Senate and the House in action and got chills in the Supreme Court.

But that acorn will stay with me the longest. It was so homely, so incongruous in that formal setting. I felt connected. A human had populated that room.

Oct. 11, 1991

FYI: I haven't been back to Washington since. I hear things have changed since 9/11, and I imagine policies are different now. What a drag.

J'Accuse

I PROMISED MYSELF I wouldn't write about the riots following the Rodney King verdict. Too many would write too much in too many places. I knew I'd see breathless ranting everywhere I looked. Not me. I'd be different.

However, a particular aspect of the subsequent disaster troubles me. I haven't seen anything about it, and it needs mentioning. Somebody better.

My years at the *Journal* taught me to recognize the hum of a Good Story.

A reporter's definition of a good story is probably different than yours. Kindness and gentleness have nothing to do with it. A good story's exciting. It's different. It says something. It exposes something. Good stories make reporters. Best of all—and most important—good stories sell papers.

I could imagine the champing at the bit in the city rooms and TV news departments around the state. The excitement! The adrenaline rush! The race to get information *now*, get it *right*, write it *quick* and get it *first!*

So everybody jammed the Los Angeles streets following the verdict. Everybody: the local TV stations as well as CBS, NBC, ABC, CNN; the local papers as well as the bigger city papers; as well as UPI, AP, *USA Today, Time, Newsweek.* Everybody. I'm not exaggerating. You saw them, too.

Every time I saw film of looters ransacking a store, I saw photographers taking pictures of them.

I know that a rioter dragged a truck driver out of his vehicle and beat him. The camera operator in a TV network helicopter caught this, saw a Good Story—*wow*, exulted the news director—and filmed it as it happened.

I know that the curfew was violated. The TV reporters, breaking that curfew themselves, breathlessly told us about it as they clogged the streets with spotlights and video cameras and got in the way of the cops and the firefighters.

I even know that the police had beaten up King. The media had shown that tape to me, and you, all of us, over and over and over. Not the whole minute and a half; just the five seconds, those most incendiary, horrifying five seconds that guaranteed a Good Story.

I know, I know. One makes one's own decision to loot, break windows, set fires, hurt people and attack policemen.

But in this age of 15-minute fame, the presence of a TV camera encourages a look-at-me bravado that might not show itself were no media representative in sight.

Evidence: the foolishness of people at sporting events when they realize the camera's on them; demonstrations that heat up when the participants realize the camera's on them; the self-conscious rage of that rioter as he aimed his last kick at that truck driver—it looked like he kicked for the camera, *because the camera was on him.*

The media would like us to think they are a mirror of society, not part of society.

Yeah. Sure they do. But it ain't necessarily so.

By virtue of their presence, the media can alter news all by themselves. As viewers, we are encouraged to forget this. We forget that a group we see videotaped on a news broadcast isn't just any motley group of people behaving a certain way.

No—this is a group of people behaving a certain way *with a TV camera on them.*

And that camera isn't filming all by itself. There's no cold, impersonal recording machine here. Someone with his own baggage, his own prejudices, his own hunt for a Good Story decides where to aim that camera, chooses what we see. Or somebody else tells him where to aim it—someone with his own baggage and prejudices.

By meticulous, premeditated selection of these electronic images, the media can work to calm us down or heat us up. But if we calm down, we have no reason to keep watching. And if we stop watching, what happens to all that happy ad revenue?

Abetting is a crime. Inciting to riot is a crime. I blame the media for provoking the appalling fracas following the Rodney King verdict. That deadly uproar was the direct, predictable result of their idiotic, reckless hunt for ratings, viewers and sponsors.

It's a great reason—one of many—to kill your television.

May 14, 1992

Forty—the Beginning of the End

A LONG TIME AGO, when my heartthrob of the moment ran out of sweet nothings to murmur in my ear about June, the moon, the sun, the stars and the purple mountain's majesty reflected in my eyes, he moved on to what he'd do when he turned 40.

At 40, the age that signifies the beginning of the end, he would kill himself. At 40, he said, decrepitude would have caught up with him, and the inevitable deterioration ahead would make further existence pointless. Whatever meager pleasure he'd get out of life would be overshadowed by his body's inescapable, inevitable and inexorable push toward decay.

How old was he then? Older than I, 25 I'll bet, certain in his plan, solemn and earnest in his theory.

I found his intention courageous and clear-sighted, far more courageous than mine. My plan? My plan involved living until I fell apart and my heart stopped on its own. This had nothing to do with any deep thinking, however. Instead, I was lazy, content to rely on inertia—I was living, so I'd continue doing so until acted on by an outside force.

Plus, I was chicken.

Sure, he snorted. You're too chicken to die but not too chicken to endure hardening of the arteries, loss of memory, sight, hearing and bowel control, the desolation of repulsive wrinkles and the inevitable indignity of age, all fates worse than death. All, he assured me, would attack at 40.

The last time we discussed this, we drove from Redding to Eureka on Highway 299, a road that twists along the Trinity River through mountainous country studded with pines and cottonwoods. Periodically, I pointed out the red-tailed hawks in the brilliant blue sky and the shadows of trees darkening the water that tumbled whitely over the granite.

Sure, I agreed, you need full dentures when you're 43, diapers at 57 and you're bent double at 61. But even though you're feeble and ailing, couldn't you still enjoy stuff like all that wet granite? And what about poppies and lupine in the spring, and the changing colors in fall, and books? Not to mention Cary Grant movies?

Irrelevant, he sniffed. A pleasant fantasy. I might kid myself, but not him. At 40 he'd be gone. No hairy ears for him.

At the risk of understating the case, I understand now how little we understood then. All our impressions of age came from the outside looking in. In our early 20s, sure of our intelligence, we were convinced we understood what we saw.

But neither of us had any idea. We had no room in our impressions to imagine the various amazing phenomena waiting for us. Then, the only people we felt comfortable associating with were others the same age. We couldn't envision a dear friendship with someone 40 years older or 20 years younger. We had no idea of the joy and depth—the gift—of a 60-year friendship, not to mention a marriage of that length.

We believed that the convictions we held to be self-evident at

23 or 25 would remain self-evident. Certain of our certainties, sure we were the best we could be—the best anyone could possibly be—we believed that there wasn't much left for us to learn. We knew we knew the truth. And we knew we knew what the truth was.

We believed that one always knew when one was old. We believed that with the unavoidable clues of bifocals, crepey skin, thinning hair, expanding waistline, creaky bones and a lingering affection for Jack Benny—whoever he was—how could you not know? Surely you'd see that incriminating evidence.

If he's still alive, my erstwhile pal is nearing 50. I wonder if he still considers that view he held with such intensity and so intensely 25 years ago. I wonder if he still plans to kill himself when he gets old... and when he thinks that will happen.

April 21, 1994

Let's Scare the Pants Off Them

A FTER WEEKS OF *listening to the media harangue us, getting more and more shrill about anthrax and the threat of terrorism after Sept. 11:*

"…And next we have Sam at the White House. Yes, Sam?"

"Hello Jack, yes, I'm here at the White House where the president has urged patience. While the situation is, as he says, a getting worse, he stresses that we shouldn't panic. Earlier today, as they did yesterday, the day before that and the day before that, the head of the FBI and the attorney general both said that the worst thing we can do as a nation is panic. Everyone I've talked to urges the media to use restraint in our reporting of these stories. They insist that the worst-case scenarios are just that, worst-case scenarios."

"That's a good point, Sam. Overreacting is just playing into the hands of the enemy. There's no need for panic, even as it becomes obvious that our leaders don't have a clue how to solve the problem, and we should all start stockpiling antibiotics and taking them as a preventative measure. Stay tuned for updates on that unsettling story… Yes, I'm told we have Tom in the field. Tom?"

"Hello, Jack, yes, I'm here at the Ringling Brothers laboratory, the country's largest pharmaceutical manufacturer. Their spokesman says that because they were caught off guard, they may not have enough chemicals to manufacture the correct dosage of antibiotic necessary to serve the millions of people who might need it in the next several weeks."

"So there might not be enough antibiotics for everyone if an anthrax epidemic does happen to occur?"

"That's right, Jack, but then again—"

"Thank you very much, Tom. Viewers, be sure to stay tuned for updates on that terrifying story. And remember not to panic. Meanwhile, Sally has some comments about survival techniques. Sally?"

"Hello, Jack, yes, tonight I'm discussing what to do if your neighbor has smallpox. Whatever you do, don't go next door. Instead, rip out the number nine insulation from behind your walls and water it down—but only if you have sterilized mineral water. If you spray number nine insulation with ordinary tap water, you'll release poisonous argon-15 gas into the air."

"Sally, would you tell our viewers what they should do if they don't have number nine insulation behind their walls?"

"Well, Jack, if that's the case they should go outside and lick their neighbor's door knob."

"So—nothing they can do, eh? Thank you very much, Sally. Stay tuned for updates on that frightening story. Remember, there is no need to panic. I said, there is no need to PANIC.

"Now, visiting with us in the studio is Dr. Hal Credershran, an expert on poisons at the Amalgamated Center for Prevention of a Terrified Citizenry Going Off Half-Cocked. Dr. Credershran, we've heard many horrifying rumors—rumors that we're probably irresponsible for spreading—really grisly rumors about smallpox germs being used as germ warfare.

"How likely is this, Dr. Credershran, and how difficult would it be to spread over a wide area?"

"Hello, Jack, yes, I think it's extremely likely that a terrorist group could get hold of smallpox. However there's an even deadlier weapon out there that can be disseminated much quicker and easier than smallpox. Just shred paper bags into dust, add India ink, Old Spice aftershave and artichoke leaves, pour the mixture into a spray bottle and spray away."

"So you're telling our viewers that inhaling this lethal mixture results in an illness more deadly than smallpox, and that its imminent dissemination is a distinct possibility?"

"Yes, but I don't think there's any cause for alarm."

"Thank you, Dr. Credershran. Be sure to stay tuned for updates on that horrifying story. And please remember, there is no need to panic. Finally, Cookie has a report about suspicious behavior."

"Hello, Jack, yes, the president has asked us all to watch for suspicious behavior. The experts all agree that anything out of the ordinary is suspicious—people who don't fly the American flag, or who don't know the words to "The Star-Spangled Banner." Especially suspicious would be people who purchase Old Spice aftershave, have paper bags in their garages or spray bottles in their laundry rooms."

"Thank you, Cookie. Viewers, be sure to stay tuned for updates on that terrifying story. And please remember, everyone, there is NO NEED TO PANIC. Let me say that again: There is NO NEED—"

Meanwhile, in a walnut-paneled boardroom filled with Emmy awards and high-ranking network executives: "Well, the figures are still dismal.

Revenues are rotten. We won't climb out of the red until we can make up the millions we lost by not airing any commercials those days after Sept. 11."

"We're doing the best we can. We've assured advertisers that we'll continue scaring the pants off the public so they'll keep watching. The more they watch, the more frightened they get, and the more frightened they get the more they watch—and the more ads they'll see and the more money they'll spend. Not to worry. There is no need to panic."

###

Oct. 25, 2001

Ways to Greet the New Year

O NE OF MY favorite New Year's Eve memories has nothing to do with me, except by association. When my sister was about 5, she tagged along with my mother to the little neighborhood grocery store in the chill early evening of Dec. 31. Mother needed to do some last-minute stuff she'd forgotten about earlier in the day, or that she only now was finding the time to deal with. You know. You've been there.

It was dark. Time to be home, for heaven's sake, they had other things going on. Mother was tired, cold, harried, and she'd hardly thought about dinner. From the number of cars in front of the store, she knew she'd find others in there facing the same situation: people wanting to be someplace else. Sigh.

But my sister saw this dark New Year's Eve differently. In her scuffed-up red rubber rain boots and her green sweatshirt and her uneven blonde bangs, she burst through the swinging doors with her arms raised and shouted "HAP-py New Year!"

Mother took great pleasure from that story, always telling it with her face wreathed in delight. She was tickled not only by her daughter's enthusiasm and generosity, but also by the reaction of those in the checkout line: They were tickled, too. The night became less dark, less cold, and the idea of a new year just around the corner became a welcome thing. Rather than old hat, rather than a disconcerting symbol of the inexorable march of time—*What, January again, already? Another year older and deeper in debt*—suddenly this New Year's Eve became exciting, full of magic.

I think about that gleeful little girl barreling through the doors whenever I step out the doors by myself at midnight on New Year's Eve, toasting this old earth as it careens around the sun, doing its own version of bashing through the swinging doors. Yet for such a big beast, it moves so quietly into the new year.

It's the rest of us who make all the noise.

I have some New Year's resolutions for y'all to think about before we burst into 2003. I hate New Year's resolutions for myself, because if I make them I usually break them. So I don't make them publicly. Instead, I have resolutions for other people.

For everyone who emails spam with oh-so-hilarious jokes: Resolve to consider that it's possible that some might not think they're funny. Especially jokes that put down men, Iraqis, people who play badminton or who aren't Christian. Would it be OK with you if someone emailed jokes putting down people like you?

For everyone who has an argument to make: Resolve to believe that it's possible that your opponents are not stupid. Just because your opponents don't agree with you doesn't make them cretins. Resolve to refrain from insulting your opponent as a way of making your point.

For everyone worried about the government's apparent interest in invading your privacy via the Homeland Security Bill: Resolve to consider saying the heck with it, and investigate John Hinckley's assassination attempt on Reagan. Or the lives of Bernard Goetz, Ted Kaczynski and Tim McVey. Check out books on atomic power and communism and the Koran and Castro. This is, of course, in addition to all the other books you take home—the ones focusing on John Adams, genealogy, orchids, rebuilding tractor engines, ragtime, quilts, dachshunds, *Cat Who* mysteries and how to make beer—along with all those back copies of *The Nation* and *Smithsonian* you already bring home.

I mean, rather than fret that the government might know what you're doing, resolve to revel in their nosiness. Give 'em something to talk about while showing them they can't prevent you from investigating what you want to investigate. And then maybe, since you won't be whispering anymore, no one will pay any attention. And think of the education you'll give yourself!

For those who still believe that the camera doesn't lie: Resolve to become educated about the endless and unnerving possibilities of seamless digital manipulation in this information age. A photo is making the rounds of George Bush earnestly and sternly looking through a pair of binoculars—with the lens caps still on. Amusing, of course, but please be aware that somebody who knows how inserted those lens caps on the computer.

And resolve with me to be the change you wish to see in the world. Heck, why not let it start here?

HAP-py New Year!

Dec. 26, 2002

Acknowledgements

ONCE UPON a time, I eyed those acknowledgements at the back of books with skepticism. If a person is a decent writer, I thought, why on earth would she need all that help?

I also remember feeling equally dubious each time I read the end of *Adventures of Huckleberry Finn:* "If I'd a knowed what a trouble it was to write a book I wouldn't a tackled it," Huck grouses, "and I ain't a-going to no more."

Oh come on, I scowled, from the outside looking in. All it takes to write a book is the wherewithal, an idea, time and skill. And if you have those, why on earth would it be so much trouble?

Well. I know better now. As I write this from the inside looking out, please believe me: This project has not been a solitary effort.

Writers on the Storm (WOTS), former students of mine who have created their own group, have been relentlessly supportive and enthusiastic.

SuRFerS (Susan Rushton's Former Students—a name I'm honored by but one I didn't create) have been relentlessly supportive and enthusiastic.

Gold Country Writers (goldcountrywriters.com) have offered me a bunch of role models and people to go to for advice.

The Placer County Writers' Group has also offered me a bunch of role models and advice.

I invited some friends to my editing bee (think cornhusking, quilting bee, barn-raising) and several took me up on it. Each pored over several columns and found things that I could no longer see. I value the time, the vision and the observations of Chery Anderson, Adonna Gipe, kW Rice, Ed Weiss, Barbara Gerletti-Weiss, Linda Frederick Yaffe and Penni Smith.

Penni Smith is also my webmaster (thewordandweb-smith.com). I thank her for her skill, and for insisting that I get myself technologically competent. Both of us will always be disappointed in me along those lines. But I value her patience and encouragement.

Thanks to Norma Lehr, Bob Snyder, Persia Woolley and Linda Frederick Yaffe for agreeing to tell you how wonderful they think I am (on the back cover).

Vance Sauter (goldtripub.com), the genius who created the book cover, has been endlessly patient and helpful. I appreciate his recommendation of Michael Kirby (kirbyphoto.com), who took the cover photos. I thank Michael, too—for his skill, enthusiasm and patience.

You've no doubt noticed, as I certainly have, that sharp-eyed people brimming with skill and patience, enthusiasm and friendship surround me. How lucky for me. And how grateful I am.

And of course I thank my husband Don. I know, you see people thanking their spouses all the time at the end of these things. But I could not have accomplished this project without him—without his enthusiastic support; his infinite, happy and patient patience; and without his engineer's eye and skill. Thank you, Mr. Rushton. You're my favorite work of art.

Another copy of this book
is waiting for you at

mootpointpress.com

Also available in ebook form.
Please investigate!

16926010R00199

Made in the USA
Charleston, SC
17 January 2013